The Lady Who Chose Joy

Beauty from the Ashes

CAROL JOY POWERS

Poem by Barbara Sturgess.

I have depended on my memories and stories shared with me by Elsie's family members and her Friends. I make no explicit guarantees about the accuracy of the information contained in this book. Dialogue is included but I do not guarantee the exact words, or that the order of events are correct.

Family photos property of Carol Joy Powers.

Cover photo by Foundry via Pixabay.

Formatted by Katie Erickson, KatieEricksonEditing.com.

ISBN: 978-0-9668622-4-9

Dedication

This little book is dedicated to the honor and glory of God in memory of my mother, Elsie, who loved Him with all her heart.

"… to comfort all who mourn; … to give them beauty for ashes, the oil of joy for mourning, the garment of praise for the spirit of heaviness… that He may be glorified."

Isaiah 61:2b-3 NKJV

Acknowledgments

Many thanks go to my husband for encouraging me to write this story and to my daughters. Gayla for her help in proofreading it, Jannelle for the work she did in discovering some of the details prior to the families migrating to America and Canada. And to my son, Ted, who gave me many hours of help with the computer and helped prepare the original pictures so they could be printed. And especially Bobbie Bomar Brown who so kindly read it and offered many helpful suggestions.

Table of Contents

Prologue 1

Before the Beginning 3

Chapter One 9

Chapter Two 29

Chapter Three 41

Chapter Four 49

Chapter Five 71

Chapter Six 85

Chapter Seven 93

Chapter Eight 113

Chapter Nine 131

Epilogue 135

Useful References 139

A Bit of the Rest of the Story 143

Exquisite Moment 203

About the Author 219

Prologue

My great-grandfather Daniel's ancestors were being oppressed, not only that, but these people were also struggling to provide for their families in their homeland of Germany. In 1763 word came to them that Catherine the Great wanted people to settle in her recently acquired areas of Southern Russia.

She knew that most of the Germans were very industrious workers and conscientious people. She sent word that if any of these families would come to settle there and establish homes and farms in these unsettled areas, she would give them free land. The people who chose to accept her offer would not have to pay any taxes, their sons would not have to serve in the military, and she would even give them a small amount of money to help them start their new lives in Russia. The best part was that everyone would have freedom to worship as he or she wanted. Since most Germans at that time were either Baptist or Lutheran and the Russians were mostly Russian Orthodox this was very appealing. It all sounded too good to be true.

Little by little a few brave families decided to accept this offer and when these families got to southern Russia, they discovered that it was all true and soon letters were sent back to their families and friends in Germany. It was not long before there was a rather large migration of German immigrants to that area of southern Russia, the part which today we know as Ukraine. These German immigrants settled together in their own communities, continued to speak German, worshipped as each one wanted, and everyone worked hard. Their farms prospered, their sons did not have to serve in the military, and none of these people paid any taxes. They formed their own little German communities. It was just like the good times which these folks had enjoyed before the oppression started in Germany. This truly became home to them, and they loved and were happy in their new country.

Daniel was born and grew up during these good times. During those years he met and married Katrina whose ancestors had also immigrated from Germany. Daniel and Katrina established their own prosperous farm and soon had three little boys of their own.

The good times lasted just over one hundred years then things began to change. There were new rulers in Russia. The new rulers liked that the motherland of Russia had been well cultivated and well-established by the German farmers, but the Russian people began to resent that these immigrants did not pay taxes and their sons did not serve in the military. These immigrants did not worship in the Russian Orthodox way. Soon it became obvious that the too-good-to-be-true offer was not so good anymore. Things began to change quickly, and it became obvious that these immigrants would have to either comply with the new rulers' wishes or they would have to emigrate somewhere else.

Many chose to emigrate to America or Canada and in these two countries, these German immigrants found real freedom.

Before the Beginning

What should we do? Katrina and Daniel had numerous lengthy discussions agonizing about what would be best for them to do. The concern that their home country, Russia, was no longer a safe and peaceful place to live had become a genuine reality. There were small wars in various locales, rumors of bigger wars, taxes were going up remarkably high, and prices were going up. It was harder and harder to get the farming supplies they needed. Neighboring young men were being conscripted and forced to join the military and fight in the various wars.

Daniel and Katrina had three small boys and were worried about a secure future for their family. Russia just did not feel safe there anymore. It was very hard to think about selling everything they had worked so hard to acquire. It would be even harder to leave all their families and everything familiar behind, but their Russian home could not begin to compare with the many good things which had been learned about America.

America was called the land of opportunity. There was good fertile land at cheap prices. Life would be a peaceful and happy one there. Life would be safer for their growing boys; and the young men would not be conscripted to serve in the military against their will. Most importantly everyone would be free to worship as he or she felt they should, and the family would be safe again. Neither Daniel nor Katrina knew how to speak the language of America but determined that they would learn. Finally, it was decided the best thing for their family would be to immigrate to America. Their farm was sold, their farm equipment and all their belongings were also sold to raise the money for boat tickets so the entire family could go to America.

Choosing to settle in an area of South Dakota because there were several other German-speaking families there and thinking it would feel more like home to them to be among other people like themselves the decision was finalized to move to South Dakota. Yes, their clothes were a bit different than their American neighbors, some of their customs were different than those who had been in America for a longer time, sometimes they were laughed at, and they did not speak the language, but they were young, and vowed to learn as quickly as possible.

Daniel was a good farmer and worked very hard, Katrina was a true helpmeet for him. As soon as possible they began to acquire some farm animals and with God's blessing and hard work their farm prospered. In 1893 a little girl was born to them, and they named her Lydia. She was the first baby born to them in America. Shortly after Lydia's birth, Katrina died, and Daniel was alone with his three boys and little daughter. He felt so alone and was lonesome. He soon realized that he needed a companion for himself and someone who would be a good mother to his children.

Then he thought of Carolina. She was a cousin of Katrina's. She was also a good, kind-hearted young lady and he knew that she would be a good help to him and would lovingly care for his children, so they were married. Daniel and Carolina chose to move to North Dakota, and then lived there for several years. Then many interesting stories began to come to them. Canada is better. There is free land to homesteaders who improve the land. There are large wide-open spaces waiting to be cultivated. The land is very fertile, and you can have big farms. Daniel and Carolina began to discuss these opportunities with some nearby neighbors who were their best friends.

When Lydia was 15, Daniel put their cattle and tools into a box car and shipped them north to Canada. The family and the neighboring families who had also chosen to make this move to Canada rode in covered wagons. This small group of friends decided to settle on the prairies of Alberta.

The first winter after the family had arrived in Canada, they had no house to live in. Places were quickly prepared to protect their animals from the cold, but there was not sufficient time to build houses for themselves, therefore, Daniel and Katrina's family spent the whole first winter living in tents! It was COLD but they survived. They always worked awfully hard.

Daniel and Carolina had a good and happy life together. One more daughter was born to them. She was born just a year before Lydia got married. The boys all helped Daniel plant crops and the crops did well. Houses were built and the children grew. The years passed quickly, and Lydia had become a young lady.

In that same farming community in Alberta, there was another German family whose ancestors had migrated to Russia to take advantage of Catherine the Great's offer. This mother and father had two boys and two girls. By 1884 this family also realized that it would be better for them if they left Russia. The father of this family was named Adam Roth, upon arriving in America, he chose to settle in South Dakota. There Adam and his wife had two more sons born to them. The first was a boy whom they named Christian. In German they shortened his name to Christ. Shortly after Christ's birth Adam and his wife immigrated to Canada and made Alberta their new home.

As he began talking increasingly more English and less German, Christ wanted to be called Chris, not Christ. Christ is the German nickname for Christian, but he was a kind and humble young man, and he did not want his English-speaking friends to confuse his name with the English name of Jesus Christ.

Chris was a very hard worker and he loved school. By the time he had finished the eighth grade in the local public school, he wanted more education. After talking with his parents, it was decided to send him to the closest Christian boarding school.

It was the first time Chris had been away from home, so there were many new experiences waiting for him. He was such a friendly guy that he soon had a large group of new friends. One afternoon, early in the school year three or four of his new friends invited him to walk into town with them. He was happy to have a bit of free time, so the boys walked into town. When the group was well away from the school grounds, some of the group bought some cigarettes and began to smoke. They kindly offered him a cigarette.

He was totally horrified! He absolutely wanted no part of that filthy habit and he strongly refused. But he remained with the group. After their free afternoon, the group of boys went back to the dorm.

Sometime the next day Chris was called into the principal's office. Chris could not think of anything wrong that he had done. He had no idea why he should be asked to go to see the principal, but he went. There he received the shock of his young life. The principal asked him if he had gone into town the previous afternoon. Chris answered in the affirmative, then the principal told him, "You were seen smoking, so you are expelled. You must leave the campus immediately."

Chris was devastated. He knew he had not smoked. He knew he never wanted to do such a dirty thing. He tried his best to explain to the principal that he had not smoked. The boys he was with had been smoking, they had tried to get him to join them, but he did not believe in that filthy habit. He begged and pleaded but the principal would not listen to him. Finally, the principal said, "Well, you are guilty by association, and we will not tolerate such people on our campus."

Chris sadly left school, but he had been deeply, deeply hurt. Then as he was on the train on the way home, he began to think of the injustice of it all and he became angry. So, he decided if I am not believed, if I am accused of smoking, my reputation is ruined, I may as well go ahead and smoke.

He did begin to smoke, not a lot, not always, and he must have been ashamed of it for he hid it well and none of his family or close friends knew that he was smoking. Once back on the farm Chris threw himself into becoming the best farmer he could be. His life was busy, and the years slipped by quickly. Soon there were enough German immigrants in that area that they were able to get together and build a small church in which to worship. Every week he faithfully went to church with his family and there he noticed the young lady, Lydia, who had moved to that community with her parents sometime after his parents had settled there. She also noticed him!

Chris and Lydia soon knew that there was something special about each other. In those days young people did not talk much about love. The parents arranged the marriages, so Chris and Lydia did not say much but after a while they began to talk to their parents, and both of them let their parents know they wanted to be married. Daniel and Carolina knew that Chris was a good young man, hard-working and honest, and that he loved God, so gave their blessing and permission for Lydia to marry Chris.

Chris and Lydia were married in January of 1915 and for their wedding night he was able to take her into town where they were to spend their wedding night in a real hotel, then they would move into the house he had prepared for them.

When Chris and Lydia got to the hotel room, he told Lydia, "You go ahead and get ready for bed, I am going to take a short walk and I'll be back soon." She was rather surprised but was glad for the opportunity to prepare for bed in privacy. Soon Chris was back, and he bent over to kiss her. Immediately she smelled the tobacco on his breath. She quickly backed away from him and told him, "No one who smokes will ever kiss me." That was the very last cigarette that Chris ever smoked. He knew his new wife had very firm and good principles.

Chapter One

Chris and Lydia had been married just over a year when on February 13, 1916, a baby girl joined their family, they named their baby girl Elsie. Their house just overflowed with love and happiness. Lydia now became Mama. She was a very good cook, and she made such yummy food. She made her own noodle dough and then she made kase knoepfla served with a good, sweet cream sauce and grischtla sprinkled all over the top. Today some people call them cheese pockets, and these were topped with small crispy fried breadcrumbs. Her family also liked the haloupsie (stuffed cabbage rolls) which she made. She made sweet soft cinnamon rolls, crusty homemade bread of all kinds, and fruit or cheese kuchen. They never had to go to the store to buy bread.

Mama also made delicious sour cream gravy. Sometimes there was so much cream a bit of it would go sour, other times she just let a bit go sour so that she could make sour cream gravy. Her family really enjoyed her sour cream gravy. Today her granddaughter still makes sour cream gravy, and even her great granddaughters and her great grandsons make it for their families. She prepared all kinds of fresh vegetables from her own garden. There was often a pot of savory soup simmering at the back of the large wood-burning stove.

She was a good homemaker and kept her house neat and clean. The floors had to be swept with a broom and then scrubbed by hand while she was kneeling on the floor. Elsie's little clothes were always clean and neat. Mama had to wash all the laundry by hand in a large metal tub and scrubbed on a metal wash board all by hand. Then Mama carried the clothes outside and hung them in the sunshine and fresh air to dry. The clean clothes smelled like fresh air when brought into the house. Sometimes in winter the clothes would freeze before being completely dried. After the clothes were completely dry, Mama would heat a heavy iron on the top of the wooden stove and then iron the little clothes. It was a lot of challenging work for her, but she loved taking care of her small family. Papa knew he had made an excellent choice in choosing to love and marry Mama. Often Mama said, "I'm so thankful that our marriage was a real love marriage, and not one of the arranged marriages like most of the others which happen in our community."

Papa was a very industrious worker. Before being married, he had purchased his own farm, a large one. Then he built a lovely 2-story house on it. He wanted to have a delightful home for his new bride-to-be. He put long strenuous and tedious hours and so much love into building that house just for her, for them.

He designed the second floor to have four bedrooms. Likely expecting that he and Mama would have a large family, or maybe lots of visitors, or maybe both. He constructed this home the best he could because he wanted to be prepared for whatever came. He wanted it large enough and sturdy enough to last a loving family a good long time.

One of the most special things he did was to put in a real bathroom upstairs. However, it was considered so special that when the weather was permissible, and people were able to go outside, they used the outhouse which Papa had built at the back and a little to the side of their house. It was a good outhouse; it was a two-seater! You did not have to go out there alone. If you wanted, you could have someone go with you and sit side-by-side.

The main floor had a nice large parlor. This was a special room and would have a large comfortable sofa, several good chairs, and a piano because Papa loved to sing. The parlor was used for special occasions and where their guests could be entertained. The family could also use it in the evenings to have worship or other special family times. The house also had a dining room, one big enough that it held a dish cabinet and a table large enough for the whole family and even their guests to all sit around and eat together. They would have many good times and delicious meals sitting around this table. Right off the dining room, at the front of the house, would be Mama's and Papa's bedroom. Behind the living room and dining room there was a large kitchen with a nice big pantry. Papa wanted it to be pleasant and easy for Mama to work there.

Papa had a big wood-burning iron stove put into the kitchen for her. He also dug a large well and put a big windmill over it, then he dug ditches and put in the pipes so that Mama would have water running right into her kitchen. She did not have to go out to the well and carry her water in, it was right there at the kitchen sink. Papa was so thoughtful of Mama.

The kitchen had two sections. One part was where she prepared the food and washed the dishes. It had a good-sized countertop so she could knead the bread, roll out the kuchen, chop vegetables, and prepare other delicious dishes. Right under the window, she had a big rectangular sink where she washed the vegetables she was going to prepare and the dishes that had been used. At the end of that part of the kitchen there was a large pantry where Mama could keep her flour, sugar, salt, and other large and small staples which she would use daily. She could also keep the butter and cream in there, plus baked bread, cookies, kuchen, and other baked goodies. It also was a place for her to store her mixing bowls, miscellaneous utensils, and kettles. Mama was a neat person, and she kept a clean, well-organized kitchen.

The other part of the kitchen had the stove. Papa also added a wash-up sink to this part of the kitchen. It was close to the back door where he could wash his hands and face when he came in from working out in the fields and there was a small table by a side window where the young family often ate at noon.

Downstairs there was a large basement where Mama could store all the lovely food she had canned for the winter. It was a perfect place to keep the large pickle keg, the sauerkraut barrel, some of their potatoes, beets, carrots, cabbage, and other vegetables so that she did not have to go outside in the cold and snow to the underground cellar every day. Papa was so thoughtful of Mama; he did everything he could to make her life easy. He wanted her to be happy.

Across the front of the house was a porch where Papa hoped he and Mama could sit and relax in the evenings after the work was done. Even though the porch faced north, they could see the sun go down when they were sitting there. It was very welcoming to any guests who might come visiting.

In the back of the house was an enclosed porch where Papa and anyone who had been working outside could leave their dirty clothes, shoes, or boots before coming into the house. It would help Mama keep the kitchen floor clean. She had to scrub it all by hand, so he was very thoughtful to put this large area right next to the kitchen door. From that porch there was a door and steps leading to the outside. In the summer this was a good place for Mama to store the eggs until it was time to take them to town.

He did not build this delightful house out of pride, but out of his special love. It ended up being the nicest house for miles around in that part of the country. The neighbors were happy and glad for them because they were such a loving couple and always so kind and helpful to everyone in their community.

The days flew into weeks and the weeks became months. Mama always kept Elsie close by her side and Elsie's little eyes watched everything Mama did. Soon Elsie was toddling around, and she loved to follow her dear Mama wherever she could. She was Mama's little shadow and Mama was always so kind and patient with Elsie.

The happy days just seemed to melt into one another because there was so much love and it seemed that the next day could hardly wait to arrive with something else interesting to do. With such a large farm and a young baby there was always a lot of work to be done. There were days it was discouraging, some days it seemed they would not get it all done, but they always did what they had to do cheerfully, lovingly, and happily. Mama and Papa did not use angry, cross, or harsh words in their home. Their words were kind and loving words. In the small community where they lived, it seemed that everyone always knew everyone else's comings, goings, doings, and anything else that happened. Mama's friends noticed her content and cheerful home and she would often shyly tell them, "Our marriage was a real love marriage. It was not an arranged marriage like so many others." At that time, people did not talk much about love, so she was a bit shy to talk openly about their love.

Soon spring came and Papa was busy planting his crops and Mama was busy putting in her garden, keeping the clothes clean, and cooking meals for Papa and the men he had to hire to help him with all the work it took to keep a large farm running smoothly. Then summer followed with all its busy work out on the farm and Mama was busy canning corn, green beans, tomatoes, and lots of other good food for wintertime. Late summer and early fall followed quickly and that is when the farm crops were harvested. Winter was also a busy time because Papa was busy mending the horses' harnesses, sharpening his tools, getting everything ready for planting-time next spring. The days were longer and much colder, so Elsie stayed inside during most of the winter. It was always a busy time and so much to do and always done with so much love.

No matter what season of the year it was, Papa was always busy. He was a very diligent and industrious worker and of course the cows had to be milked every morning and every evening, no matter what time of the year it was and how much other work there was to do. The horses had to be fed and groomed, the barn mucked out, meaning he had to clean out all the manure which the animals had made. That was not so pleasant, it was stinky and lots of work, but he always took the best care of his animals. He kept them and the barn clean, just like Mama kept the house clean. When it was haying time and the hay had been cut it had to be brought into the barn and put up into the loft (the upstairs part of the barn). That was a lot of hard physical work. Then in the winter he had to go up into the loft and throw the hay down for the animals to eat. Who knew life could be so busy and so full of love?

By the second springtime Elsie was old enough to follow Mama and watch her plant the seeds in her garden. Mama explained that soon there would be little green leaves sprouting up out of the brown earth. They would have fresh little green lettuce leaves, lovely bright red radishes, long orange carrots, bright red tomatoes, long green beans, red beets, and bright green peas. So many good things to eat. They would also have cabbages, potatoes, and onions, to add to the beets and carrots which they had picked and stored in the cellar so that they could have healthy food to eat not only in the summer but in the winter also.

Another thing Elsie liked to do was follow Papa into the barn. The animals were so interesting to her. But there were many places where a little girl could get hurt in that big place with all the cows, large horses, and farm equipment. So, Mama and Papa were always incredibly careful when she came to the barn with them. It was fun for Elsie to watch the cows when it was milking time. Elsie also loved the kittens that were part of the barn as they helped to keep the mice away. It was always fun to watch Papa squirt a bit of milk directly into the kitties' mouths as he was milking the cows.

After Papa finished milking the cows, Mama took the milk into the separator house. This was a small building close to the barn and there she separated the milk from the cream. Oh, the milk tasted so good and sweet, and the cream was extra special. It was so thick and creamy. It made such good, sweet butter. Elsie liked to watch Mama take the cream and pour it into the butter churn. The butter churn was like a little round barrel, it had a cover over the top and in the top was a wooden handle which had a paddle at the bottom end. After the cream was in the barrel, Mama would pull the handle up and then push it down. It went up and down, up and down, and up and down for a long time and finally it became the pretty golden butter that tasted so good on many of the yummy things Mama made to eat.

Elsie followed Mama into the hen house and watched her carefully gather the fresh eggs into a basket. She did not want to break any of them. Mama had to do this every day. The family would use a good deal of the eggs for themselves, and to help feed the men that Papa hired to help him with all the work on his large farm. The eggs she did not use for their family she would take into town, along with the extra butter which she did not need. The storekeeper would take some of her eggs and butter and then she could trade them for some of the things the shopkeeper had that she could not make on the farm. She could trade for fabric, salt, sugar, thread, or ever so many other little treats. Sometimes the people in town who did not have their own chickens or cows would just ask her if they could buy any extra eggs, butter, or cream from her. The people knew that Mama's butter, cream, and eggs were always fresh and clean. This provided a bit of extra cash which was always welcome.

Mama and Papa were so proud of their little Elsie. Every week the three of them got ready and Papa hitched the horses to the buggy then off they went to the little church about a mile down the road from their house. At home Mama and Papa were careful to teach Elsie about Jesus and His love. As Elsie got a little older, she loved going to church with Mama and Papa. In the early 1900's there were no special classes for children, especially in smaller churches, but it was just good to be with Mama and Papa and to see some other children who were her age. Church was a special place for her, and she learned to love Jesus and going to church with other believers.

Another thing that Mama and Papa did was always return an honest tithe to God and to give generous offerings. When the crops, butter, cream, or eggs, were sold, Papa and Mama tithed the money they received. If the produce, crops, butter, cream, or eggs were used by their family, they knew the value of these things and then tithed the value of what had been used in their home. It seemed that the more they gave to God, the more blessings they received from Him. Mama and Papa did not give to God just to receive His blessings but because they loved Him so much and therefore it was considered a privilege to always give generously. They also gave Elsie a few pennies to put into the offering plate so that she, too, would learn to give her offering when the plate was passed. Mama and Papa taught Elsie that Jesus loves her and because of that she should love Him and do what she could for him, including giving offerings when the opportunity came.

Papa and Mama's farm was at the crossroads of two country roads, and they chose to donate a corner of their land right where the roads met so that a church school could be built there. It was a small country school, but the neighbors helped to build it, and everyone was happy that their children would have a nice church school to attend. Mama and Papa wanted the best facilities possible for Elsie and any more children that might join their family someday. Their children would just have to go out the back door, walk across the yard, slip through the bushes that grew along the fence, and would arrive at the school.

The children were all in one room and there was one teacher. There was a nice large map on the wall so the children could see where the other countries which the teacher was teaching them about were located in the world. There were also some books which were shared by passing them down to the younger children for their use the next year, and there was a good-sized blackboard where they could practice their arithmetic problems. Mama and Papa wanted to have the best school that it was possible to provide for Elsie and for the other children in their community. When Elsie started to go to school, she would quickly do her lessons and when her schoolwork was done, she enjoyed listening to the lessons of the older children. She loved to read, and she loved to learn.

A young lady was hired to teach in the school and the community children were happy in their little school. The children and their parents loved their teacher and having their own school. The children enjoyed learning about so many new and interesting things and far-away places. It was also fun to plan programs for special occasions like Christmas. Most of all they enjoyed the fun at recess time with their friends. Since all the children came from farms and had lots of work to do helping at home, this short free time to play with friends was appreciated by everyone.

One day when Elsie was little over a year and a half old, she looked for her mama but could not find her. She soon found that Mama was in bed. This was not normal; Mama was always busy working. Then Elsie peeked into Mama's room and when Mama saw her, she called Elsie to come to her. What a surprise!

There in Mama's arms was a tiny baby. Mama and Papa had another healthy strong baby daughter. Both of them were glad and thankful that she was healthy. She was a welcome addition to their family and chose to call her Irene. They were sure she would always be a happy addition to their home.

Oh, she was so very cute. She was so tiny Elsie did not know whether she should touch the baby or not. But Mama said, "Elsie, this is your new baby sister. Her name is Irene. We will always love her and be kind to her. Now you are a big sister and I know you will love her and help me to take loving care of her."

Now Mama was even busier than she had been, but it was a happy busy. Again, the days melted into weeks, and the weeks into months. Elsie loved her baby sister, and it was such fun to see her grow. Elsie loved to watch Mama give Irene a bath in the kitchen wash-up sink, she loved to watch Mama feed and dress her. She really enjoyed it when Irene would smile back at her. Then when Irene started to make cute baby sounds it was so much more fun.

It was not long until Irene could say "Mama" and "Papa." She was a happy baby and would laugh often and Elsie loved her even more. She could hardly wait for Irene to say, "Elsie." One day she did, and that was a special day. Then Irene started to crawl and toddle around. Elsie loved having her own sister to play with, not just sometimes, but every day and all the time. It was like having a live baby doll. Oh, how she loved her little sister.

Soon Irene had her first birthday and it seemed like she was growing bigger every day and there just was never enough time in one day to do all the fun things. When Elsie went to the garden with Mama, Irene would go also. She liked seeing the animals in the barn and going with Mama to gather the eggs or watching as Mama pushed and pulled the beater up and down and up and down to churn the thick cream into golden butter. There were so many things to learn about and to do. Elsie felt like a very big girl because she knew all about these things now, but it was even more special for her to watch as Irene learned about everything and to see the surprise in Irene's eyes when the good sweet white cream Mama had poured into the churn, came out good yellow butter.

One day several months later Mama and Papa were noticeably quiet, they were not happy and laughing like normal. Elsie was close to three years old, but she knew something was very wrong. Mama and Papa would talk in low voices. Then Elsie noticed that Irene was not acting like the happy little sister she knew and loved.

Soon it was obvious that Irene was sick, not just a little bit sick, but extremely sick. She did not laugh and giggle, she did not want to play, she did not want to eat, she did not want to do anything at all. Mama said Irene felt extremely hot, so she tried to wash her face with cool water, but nothing helped Irene to smile and giggle. Elsie could see that Mama and Papa were sad because she did not see their usual smiles or laughter. All of their talking was just done in whispers. Elsie did not like to see her happy Mama look so sad. Nothing seemed normal or right in their home.

Finally, Mama put Irene to bed and she and Papa did everything possible to help her, but it was soon obvious that nothing they did helped Irene to feel better. Papa had to send for the country Doctor to look at her and see what was wrong. After examining her he sadly told Mama and Papa, "I am afraid she has this bad flu that is going around now. It is all over the country. You will have to try to get her to drink a lot of water. Try to bring her fever down with cool cloths. There is not much we can do, but keep her quiet, let her get as much rest as you can, and be sure to try to get her to drink plenty of water." Then he had to leave and go to visit his next patient.

Irene grew weaker and weaker. She had no interest in anything and no energy to do anything, she did not even want to eat. Mama and Papa were doing all they could, but it was obvious that nothing either of them did helped Irene feel better. It was a hard time for all of them, but Elsie had to stay away from Irene as much as possible so that hopefully she did not get sick also. Nothing was right, all was somber, serious, quiet, and sad. All too soon Irene closed her pretty sparkling little eyes and never opened them again.

In the small community news spread fast. Neighbors came to the farmhouse to help whenever and wherever possible. Someone brought a tiny coffin. Someone dressed Irene in her prettiest dress and sadly laid her in the coffin. Then the small group made an incredibly sad trip to their little church. The minister gave a talk and friends carried Irene's coffin out to the little cemetery beside the church where it was slowly lowered into the ground. Today she is sleeping there, her tombstone has a little lamb on top of it, and she is waiting for Jesus to come and wake her up all healthy, happy, and well.

Mama, Papa, and Elsie returned to their home. Now there were just the three of them again. The little Irene who had made their house so merry would never join them again until Jesus wakes her when He comes in the clouds to wake all those who have loved Him. The house seemed so empty and lonesome.

Life on a big and busy farm keeps on moving whether the people want it to or not. Sometimes being remarkably busy and having a lot that must be done helps the family to move past their heavy sorrow.

The animals needed to be cared for every day. The cows needed to be milked, the eggs gathered, the meals prepared, the garden planted and cared for, the fields planted, and crops harvested. Elsie needed her Mama and Papa; she was lonesome without Irene. Even though Elsie still followed Mama everywhere she went, it just was not the same. She missed Irene's smiles, giggles, and happy little face. Mama and Papa tried to explain to her what had happened to Irene, but they were both so busy, and Elsie just could not understand. Would she ever be happy again? She did not really understand being sad, she just knew something was very wrong in her once incredibly happy home and she was frightened because things did not feel "right" to her. What was to happen in their home? There were too many questions.

Again, the busy months came and went. Everyone missed Irene, but every day it seemed like it did not hurt quite so much now. Then when Elsie was around four years old, she had another surprise. She was a little older and she realized something was happening and it really did.

Then one day Mama introduced her to a new baby sister. Mama and Papa had chosen to name this precious little girl Melvina, so now their family was four again. Elsie was a big sister again. She felt so happy now, but she was afraid that something would happen to Melvina like it had to Irene. Elsie loved Melvina just like she had loved Irene. No, Melvina was not the same as Irene, but she was loved just as much.

Elsie got to watch as Mama now bathed baby Melvina in the kitchen wash-up sink. She watched as Melvina grew, learned to talk, learned to walk, and tried to copy everything Elsie did. Elsie liked to hear Melvina laugh. Life became happy and joyful again. Melvina loved to follow Mama and Elsie as they went about their daily work on the busy farm. Melvina grew strong and healthy.

Elsie even got a sprinkling of freckles across her nose from being out in the warm sunshine. Mama said they were cute. Elsie was not sure about that but if Mama said so she did not mind having them. Mama said they were little love spots on her nose.

Again, the busy seasons came and went, when Elsie was 7 and a half years old, she knew something was going to happen again. And it did! One day Mama introduced Elsie and Melvina to their brand-new baby brother. Oh, what joy and happiness were in their home now! Everyone was incredibly happy to have a new baby and this time it was a boy! What a special surprise. Now Elsie had a sister and a brother, no girl could have ever been so lucky.

Mama and Papa decided to name him Archie. Now their family was five. Elsie had her Mama and Papa, a little sister, and a new baby brother. Again, she watched as he grew and learned to sit up and laugh at the funny antics of his two older sisters. Elsie and Melvina loved to make him laugh. He was the cutest little baby boy. Elsie knew that someday soon he would be following Papa around the barn just like she and Melvina followed Mama in the house and garden.

Then the big day arrived when Elsie turned eight. Mama made her a birthday cake to help celebrate. She was such a big girl, and she was a real help for Mama now that Mama had two other babies who needed her care.

A few days after Elsie turned eight, she got a bad tummy ache, it was unbelievably bad. Oh, it hurt so much! Mama did her best and did all she could to take care of it. The ache in Elsie's tummy did not go away, it would not go away no matter what Mama did. It just got worse and worse. Mama and Papa were quite worried about it, so again Papa sent for the country doctor to come to their home. When the Doctor examined Elsie, he told Mama and Papa that she had appendicitis and would need an operation very quickly.

Mama and Papa wanted to get the best medical care that was available for Elsie. They did not want the doctor to have to operate on their precious Elsie right there on the kitchen table. What if something went wrong and they lost her like they had lost Irene? Papa and Mama knew it would mean a trip to the big city and a visit to a regular hospital for the operation. Papa and Mama knew their precious Elsie needed help, and she needed it immediately. Mama arranged for one of the neighbor ladies to come to their home and take care of Melvina. The hired men would take care of the animals and the farm work. Then Papa, Mama, baby Archie, and Elsie took the train into the big city. It took most of a whole day to get there.

When the family arrived in the city, Papa and Mama quickly took Elsie to the hospital. It was so big compared to her comfortable home on the farm. Everything was very strange. It was all very frightening to her. There were many strange smells in the hospital. Men and women, she did not know were coming and going everywhere and these people were all dressed in white. There were such strange beds, so different than her comfortable bed at home. She was very frightened.

After her operation Papa came to tell Elsie goodbye. She had never been away from her dear Papa in all of her just barely eight years of life. She was in a strange place, very frightened, and she hurt so badly from her operation. Papa kindly explained to her that he had to go back to the farm. He could not stay away from his duties there for the long time it would take her to heal. Animals had to be cared for and all the other chores done. Melvina was home alone with the neighbor lady. Papa absolutely had to go back to the farm, so Elsie sadly bid Papa goodbye.

Mama told Elsie that she would stay in town with baby Archie and that she would come every day to spend some time with her That helped comfort Elsie. She would look forward to her Mama's visits every day. It would almost be like having a little bit of home with her. She was so thankful to have Mama who could stay there in the city with her.

Mama came the next day to visit Elsie but then she never came again. Elsie could not understand why Mama only came one time. She had promised to come every day. Mama always did what she said she would do. No one said anything about her Mama. The nurses took care of Elsie, they brought her food to eat, and they changed her sheets and the bandages. They gave her drinks of water, but Elsie was so very lonesome. She was also scared, she did not understand, and everything was so very strange; the bed, the food, the smells; everything was strange and frightening. Most frightening of all she wondered why Mama did not come as she had promised. Was Mama gone just like Irene had gone? Was Mama ever going to come back to be with her?

It took a whole month for Elsie's operation to heal. It was not fun! Much of the time it hurt and all of the time she was lonesome and most of the time she was afraid. Her heart was sad like when Irene had been sick. Was she going to die like Irene had? She had not seen her Papa since he said goodbye and she had only seen Mama one time. Was she always going to be alone and afraid?

Finally, the day came when the doctor told her she could go home. What good news that was! When Elsie was getting dressed, she took a peek at her tummy; it had the biggest zigzag scar all across it. It was so big, and it was red. It was UGLY! But that day Mama and Papa came to take her home. She could not ever remember being so very happy. What a joyful day it was for her, she knew they were going home, and their entire family would be together again in their own beds and in their own home where everything was familiar and friendly.

At that time, Elsie did not know, because maybe no one had talked to her about it. But when Elsie had been in the hospital for her operation, the doctor had examined Mama and told her that her heart was extremely sick. He made her a patient and put her in the hospital immediately so that he could watch her and try to help her. That is the reason why Mama did not come to visit Elsie. She could not. She had also been a patient in that same hospital. She had been a couple floors higher than where Elsie was, but just could not come down to see her. The doctor made Mama stay in bed. Just like Elsie was in bed.

Maybe the nurses were trying to keep Elsie quiet, maybe they didn't want her to cry or worry, maybe everyone just thought she was too young to understand. During those years children were not told or explained much of what went on in the adult world. Whatever the reason no one had explained anything to her. She had just been so sad, lonesome, and frightened.

Now all that was over, and Elsie was simply happy to be going home with Mama, Papa, and baby brother. Archie was nine months old now. He was growing so fast, and he was so cute. He was a very loved little boy. Before the doctor had told Mama she could go home, he told her she was not do any more heavy work as her heart was very weak. She was to be most careful what she did. He even told her not to lift baby Archie.

Mama was only thirty-one, she felt "okay," and she had a large house to care for. She had a loving husband and three small children, one a baby only nine months old. She held Archie close all the way home on the train. No one really knew what she did when she got back home on the farm the next day, but she loved her family and wanted to take care of them, and she did the best she could.

Before they had gone to the hospital, every afternoon Mama would put Archie on her bed for him to take a nap, but he would not sleep unless she would lie down beside him. So, she would take a few minutes and lie down beside him until he fell asleep. Of course, she planned to do the same again as soon as they were home. What a joyful homecoming it was for all of them. Mama, Papa, Elsie, Melvina, and baby Archie. Oh, it was so very good to be home.

The next day Papa was out working in the barn. Elsie was in the house with Melvina, Mama, and baby Archie. After a little while Mama sat down on one of the kitchen chairs. When she sat down, she said, "Elsie, quick, go call Papa and tell him I need him." Elsie could tell something was not good, so she ran as quickly as she could out to the barn to call Papa. "Papa, come quickly!"

Papa ran as fast as he could and Elsie followed right behind him, but when they got to the house it was already too late. Mama was lying on the floor, and she was not breathing. She was lying there dead. Papa picked her up as gently and lovingly as he could and carried her into their bedroom, which was right off of the dining room, and there he carefully laid her on their bed.

As soon as he could Papa advised the nearest neighbor of what had happened and in the small community word travelled fast. Soon the neighbor women began to arrive to help care for the children and to help Papa "make arrangements" for Mama.

Baby Archie cried and cried, he was so tired and needed his nap, but he would not sleep without his Mama. Someone decided to put Archie on the bed beside his Mama's body and he finally fell asleep there.

Shortly everything was arranged, and there was another sad procession to their little church just down the road from their home. The pastor had a short service and then Mama was buried in the same small cemetery where Irene was sleeping. When Elsie, Melvina, and Archie were all over 75 years old, they visited that little church with their own children. At that time, one of the older members came up to Elsie and said, "When your Mama was buried, the whole front of the church was just covered in white lilies." Later Melvina told her family, "I have always HATED lilies, I have even hated the smell of them, and I never knew why. Now I understand.

After the funeral Papa went home with his two young daughters and his baby son. Life was so hard. Life was so very, very lonesome. Their home, once so full of love and happiness, was now so empty and sad. The children missed their kind and loving Mama. The neighbors took turns coming in to help, but all of them had their own families and homes which needed their care. So, none of these women stay for very long. Elsie was so very sad, she remembered how she felt when Irene was sick, how she felt when she thought she had been abandoned in the hospital, and now her dear Mama was gone. She felt sad from her head all the way down to her tummy. Would she always be sad like this? Would she ever be happy again? Papa had a big farm to run, and it became obvious that it was just impossible for him to care for the three young children, the home, and the farm all alone. Something had to be done.

After thinking about it for a while Papa decided he would go to visit the area where Mama had been born. He knew she had family in South Dakota and there were some female cousins. He also knew that Mama's Papa had remarried a cousin of Katrina's after she had died, and they had such a happy home. Maybe he could find a cousin of Mama's and she would be a companion to him and a good mother for his children. Then his home would be happy again. So, he prepared to take a trip. He asked one of the women from church to come and take care of the children while he was gone, and the hired men would take care of the animals and do the farm chores until he got back.

Papa had never gone away before. Mama was gone and would never come back and now Papa was going. The girls did not understand it at all, and baby Archie was just too young. Then after Papa had been gone for some time, the children got a letter from him. It read like this, "Dear children, I have found a New Mama for you. We will be home soon. Love, Papa"

Chapter Two

A new Mama! Elsie was so excited she could hardly wait to meet her new Mama. Now they would be a loving family again. Finally, the day came when Papa and New Mama came riding into their yard. How happy the children were to have Papa home again. He introduced the children to New Mama, but she was a big disappointment to them. She did not look at all like their dear Mama. This new Mama looked quite different, she talked quite differently, and she certainly acted very differently.

It seemed like New Mama was not even interested in any of the children, it seemed like she just did not like them. It seemed that the children could not do anything to make her happy. She hollered at them, they had never been hollered at before, Mama had only talked kindly and lovingly to them. It seemed like New Mama was angry most of the time. She beat them, oh she beat them awfully hard and so often. The children had never been beaten before.

Since Elsie was the oldest of the three children, she had to do the largest share of the chores assigned to them and since it was often not to New Mama's liking Elsie was whipped much more often than were the other two. New Mama assigned Elsie harder and much more work than a little girl of eight should have had to do. Elsie was now told that the parlor was no place for children. Elsie was only to go in there to clean. She could not sit on the sofa or any of the chairs, she could not touch the piano under any circumstances, and she was never ever to touch any of the books.

One day when Elsie was dusting the parlor she just could not resist, and she picked up and looked through the picture book which she knew had some pictures of her own dear Mama. But what a sad surprise she had when she opened it. New Mama had torn out every single picture that had Mama in it. If the picture had Papa and Mama, she had cut out Mama from the picture. Now Elsie had nothing she could look at to remind her of her own Mama. It made her so incredibly sad. She thought New Mama was just plain mean to do that.

There was one thing New Mama could not do. On the wall in the dining room there were two large oval pictures. One of Papa and one of Mama. These two photos were their wedding portraits. Papa and Mama looked so young and so happy. New Mama dared not take those pictures down for then Papa would have noticed what she had done.

Elsie did not like oatmeal, and this was something that they had almost every morning on the farm. It was very nourishing and satisfied diligent workers for a good many hours. Mama would always tell Elsie, have just a little and then you can have some toast, kuchen, or something else. New Mama was quite different, as soon as she found out that Elsie did not like oatmeal, she said, "So you do not oatmeal? Well, you will learn to like it." Then she took everything else away from Elsie, heaped her bowl extra full of oatmeal, and said, "Eat it, that is all you will get for breakfast and nothing else." So, Elsie ate her oatmeal and then some more oatmeal. Yuk! It was so hard to choke that stuff down.

Elsie did not like peas either, and when New Mama discovered that, the same thing happened. New Mama would remove all the other food from Elsie's plate and all she got was a huge plateful of those hated peas. If New Mama discovered there was anything that Elsie did not like, the same thing happened. Elsie soon learned to keep her mouth shut and eat what was there. She decided in her mind that if she ever grew up and had any children of her own, she would teach them to eat all kinds of tasty food for she didn't want them to have to go through what she had gone through.

One day the family was having kuchen. That was such a good treat, the creamy filling sometimes topped with fruit or filled with a sweet cheese and egg custard was baked in a pan which had been lined with sweet roll dough. Someone at the table said, "I wish kuchen was just the filling and not any crust." Melvina spoke up and said, "I think the crust is good." New Mama's answer to that was, everyone eat your filling and give your crusts to Melvina. Poor Melvina had to eat all the crusts while everyone else enjoyed the delicious filling.

Archie was still a baby and Melvina was very young, so it seemed that Elsie often had to take the punishment for all of them.

It was not a privilege any more to go to the little church every week. The family only went when New Mama felt like it. When their family did get to church the children all had to sit on those hard, straight-backed wooden pews. There were no children's Sabbath schools at that time. All the of the children just had to sit with the adults. New Mama would not allow Papa's children to have any toys, no books, no pencil or paper, nothing which could help them keep quiet. New Mama would not allow any of the children to turn around, all of them just had to sit still and face straight ahead. Elsie, Melvina, and Archie were not allowed to turn around to see if something or someone interesting was behind them; none of them were even allowed turn sideways to get a sideways peek at something. New Mama could turn and talk with whomever she desired, but not the children. If Elsie turned around in church, New Mama said, "You just wait until we get home, you are going to get a good whipping when we get there. You know how you are supposed to sit in church." Why could New Mama turn around whenever she wanted to and even talk, but the children could not? Life did not seem very fair sometimes.

After they got home, while Papa was out in the barn taking care of the horses Elsie got her whipping. Oh, how it hurt! If Papa had to go farther away or was occupied somewhere else, New Mama often used a part of the horse harness to whip Elsie. Whatever she could get her hands on that she knew would hurt Elsie was a tool used to punish the young children.

Elsie learned the hard way not to tell Papa what was happening. One time she felt she just could not take any more and so she confided in Papa about her beatings. Later, when he was out in the fields, New Mama gave her one of the worst beatings she had ever had up until that time. Then she told Elsie, "That will teach you to tell stories to your Papa!" So, Elsie learned to suffer in silence and not say anything to anyone. When Elsie died at ninety-two years of age, she still had scars on her back from where New Mama had beaten her.

It wasn't too long when it became obvious that New Mama was going to have a baby. Elsie knew that soon she would have to be a babysitter along with all her other chores. How could she do all of that? When the time came for New Mama to have her baby, she told Elsie, "You cannot go to school any more you must stay home and take care of me because I have to be in bed for a whole month so I can get well." Then the baby, a little girl, was born and Elsie stayed home to take care of New Mama and help with the new baby.

In that small community, news traveled fast and soon one of the neighbor ladies came to visit and see the new baby. As soon as she saw Elsie she asked, "Why, what is this little girl doing at home, why isn't she in school with the rest of the children?"

New Mama answered, "I've just had a baby and need to stay in bed for a month to recuperate so she has to stay home and take care of me and help with the baby."

The neighbor was incensed, "You cannot keep Elsie home for a month! That child needs to be in school! If you need someone to take care of you for a month, I will move in right now and take care of you and your baby and Elsie will go to school where she belongs." And that is just what happened.

This arrangement was definitely not satisfactory for New Mama, and she was soon up and out of bed. The neighbor lady went home, and Elsie was allowed to continue attending school.

The years went by, and life seemed so hard but somehow Elsie, Melvina, and Archie kept growing. Their faces, once so happy and joyful, became sad and downcast. The once cheerful happy children, whose lives had been filled with laughter, now became silent and fearful. It seemed like life was just full of work, beatings, and sadness. Life was a big burden for them.

Within a few years' time Papa and New Mama had another little girl and then another baby boy. New Mama was immensely proud of her three children. Now it was even harder for Elsie, Melvina, and Archie. New Mama got the prettiest dresses for her girls, she let their hair grow long and she made the loveliest long curls for their straight hair, and she made the prettiest big bows for their hair.

In those days flour came in large cloth bags of fifty or one hundred lbs. People bought these large bags because the women did most of their own baking and used a lot of flour for making bread and other baked goods, for making their own noodles, and many other uses. When the flour sacks were empty, they washed them and then used the cloth for making their bloomers (underwear), slips, aprons, and dish towels. Some flour sacks had designs on them, and these were even used to make dresses.

New Mama made Elsie and Melvina dresses out of those old flour sacks, not always the prettiest designs, just whatever was handy at the time. She also made their bloomers out of old flour sacks, and she was sure to make the dresses so short that those ugly bloomers always hung out below their dresses. Elsie was so ashamed of the way she looked. New Mama said she did not have time to make curls for their straight hair, so she just turned a bowl upside down on their heads and cut straight around their heads, just above their ears, so Mama's children truly had "bowl cuts."

New Mama looked at Elsie's freckles across her nose and said, "Oh, you're so speckled it is very ugly, you look just like an ugly old turkey egg!" No more "love spots." Elsie loved to read, and she loved to go to school but New Mama told her, "You are so dumb you'll never amount to anything, and you'll never be able to learn." Elsie was so ashamed, she became shy, and she felt so very stupid.

Archie was growing and it was obvious that he had inherited Papa's lovely singing voice. Archie loved to sing. He loved music. He wanted a guitar so very badly and he finally found a used one that cost twenty-five cents. He begged Papa and New Mama for twenty-five cents so that he could buy a guitar. New Mama said, "Definitely not! We cannot afford twenty-five cents to waste on a guitar for you." So that was the end of Archie ever being given a guitar.

Elsie loved music also and she wanted to learn to play the piano. New Mama said, "No! You only go into the parlor to clean and only touch the piano to dust and clean it." New Mama's girls had piano lessons, violin lessons, and accordion lessons. Those two girls were allowed into the parlor any time they wanted to go in there. Of course, her girls got to practice their music on that piano also. New Mama even bought a lovely brand-new beautiful guitar for her own son, but he had absolutely no interest in it and put it into the corner of his bedroom and there it stayed. Archie dared not even touch it. Life just did not seem very fair to Elsie, Melvina and Archie. Why did it seem that they could not do anything to please New Mama?

In a small community where everyone knew everyone else and everyone else's business, there was an obvious difference between Mama and Papa's three children and New Mama and Papa's three children. The neighbors could often be quite outspoken. Several times, different neighbors would come to the farm or talk to New Mama at church and tell her, "You cannot treat these children like that. You cannot speak to them like that. They have done nothing to deserve the way you treat them. Please do not be so mean to them." Of course, this only made New Mama angrier, and she took her frustrations out on Elsie, Melvina and Archie.

Archie was growing also and even though he had only been nine months old when Mama died, he just knew something in the house where he lived was not right. He would become so very discouraged and then he would walk the mile down to the small graveyard by the church and find his Mama's tombstone. He would sit on her grave and cry and cry for a long time. He did not understand why but it seemed to give him comfort when he could sit by her grave and cry his sorrows out where she was buried.

Uncle John, one of Daniel and Katrina's sons, lived a few miles down the road from Mama and Papa's farm. He felt so badly for the way New Mama was treating his nieces and nephew but nothing he and his wife said helped the situation so one year he and his wife decided to buy new coats for Elsie, Melvina, and Archie for Christmas. He thought they should not always have to wear old, patched, mended raggedy clothes while New Mama's children always had nice new things. When New Mama saw the beautiful new coats, she looked at them and said, "Why you do not need these! We'll put them away until later." She put the new coats at the back of the closet, and they were not seen again until a couple of years later and then she said, "You cannot wear these things, they are way too small for you." And that was the end of something new or pretty!

When the ripening wheat was just right, Elsie and Melvina liked to pick the heads of grain and then rub the kernels in the palms of their hands to remove the hulls. Then the girls would pop the grains of wheat into their mouths and chew and chew until all the starch was gone and all that remained was a lump of gluten. Elsie and Melvina would pretend this lump of gluten was chewing gum and they would chew it until they got tired and then just spit it out. Elsie and Melvina were typical girls and they really tried hard to find ways to discover something that would be fun, and which would not cause them a beating.

Once someone gave Elsie and Melvina a real piece of chewing gum. My what luxury and how the two of them enjoyed it. A whole piece of chewing gum for their very own! It was not only to chew, but it also had a good taste and even smelled good. What a treasure they had. That piece was carefully broken in half and each girl had a small piece to chew. They felt so lucky to have that special treat! When the girls were done chewing it, the chewed pieces were carefully stuck onto the back of the bedstead post so it could be saved for another day. After several days, it would be taken off, chewed again, and then it would be stuck to the back of the bedpost again. They had done this a few times and New Mama must have become suspicious because she decided to go upstairs to make sure everything was suited to her wishes and while she was checking things out, she found the used chewing gum on the back of the bedpost. What fury! And then there was another whipping. New Mama took the gum and threw it away. Well, at least they had several times of enjoyment from it. They were able to squeeze in a tiny bit of enjoyment once in a while.

One Christmas someone gave Elsie, Melvina, and Archie each an orange as a gift. What a luxurious treat! The oranges were smelled, then carefully peeled and slowly savored one segment at a time. The children loved the sweet taste and the juice running down their throats. The oranges were chewed as slowly as possible making them last for as long as they could. When the oranges were gone, Elsie and Melvina took their peelings and hid them in the dresser drawer for later. The girls would take out a piece of peel, smell it, and oh, what happy memories it gave them of that delicious orange. It seemed as though it must be just like the fruit in heaven. Occasionally they would nibble off a little piece of the peel and hold it in their mouths as long as they could before chewing and swallowing it. That way they were able to keep the peelings for quite a while. The peelings got thoroughly shriveled up, but they still enjoyed the lingering pleasant memory. Then one day New Mama climbed the stairs, went through their drawers again and found the little remaining pieces of orange peel. Again, the wrath, the whipping, and the orange peels were thrown out to keep New Mama totally in control of everything.

Churning butter was a time-consuming task and was very tiring. New Mama decided that this was something else Elsie could do to save herself some time. So, Elsie was given the added chore of churning the butter for the family. Now it was Elsie who stood at the churn and pulled the handle up and then pushed it down. Up and down, up and down, up and down, it was boring, hard work. Churning the butter was one time when Elsie was able to be by herself. And she would think about all that was happening. Why was New Mama so harsh and so mean? She obviously loved her three children, did she not love Elsie, Melvina, and Archie? If not, why not?

Elsie's arms got extremely tired because it took quite a while for the cream to become the lovely golden sweet butter that everyone liked and all of them used. Many times, just when Elsie's arms felt like they were about to fall off, she could tell that the cream was almost butter. She was so thankful that she was almost done with that chore, but then New Mama would come into the little building where the churn was kept, and she would lift the cover and pour another pitcher full of fresh cream into the churn. This meant that Elsie would have to start all over again. Because she could not have part butter and part cream, it all had to done evenly to have a nice batch of butter. So, again, her arms would go up and then down, up and down, up and down, until she was sure that her arms were certainly going to fall off. Elsie worked so hard, and she really tried to please New Mama and do everything that she was told to do. Did New Mama add more cream just to be mean and make it harder for Elsie? She dared not protest, nor could she ask. But she wondered whether New Mama did that on purpose just to make her work harder. Or to be deliberately mean? Elsie tried hard to think kind thoughts about New Mama, but it was so hard.

Another task Elsie was assigned was washing the dishes at the large kitchen sink where food was prepared. New Mama would dry them so that she could be sure all the dishes and pots and pans were cleaned to her liking and as fast as she thought they should be done. New Mama kept the solid wooden rolling pin on the counter where it was convenient for her to use in making many of the things she liked to make. If Elsie did not wash and rinse the dishes quickly enough and New Mama had to wait for anything, she would pick up that wooden rolling pin and whack it across the top of Elsie's head while she scolded Elsie for being such a lazy, slow worker. At least one wooden rolling pin was broken over Elsie's head in that manner.

Papa owned a big farm and during harvest time he hired up to 13 men to come in and help him with the harvest. Of course, all of these men had to be fed large meals because they worked hard. They often had oatmeal because it was cheap and very filling, and that full feeling lasted a long time. The men ate heartily and were given other good nourishing food to eat along with the oatmeal. But the oatmeal had to be cooked in a large metal kettle over that wood-burning stove. It would get stuck hard to the bottom of the kettle and was even harder to clean off. It was hard for a grown woman to clean but for a young girl it seemed almost impossible to do.

Elsie loved to go to school, she loved to read, and she loved her kind teacher. She really enjoyed learning about faraway places, and it was so good to be with her friends and be free from the ugly harsh words and hard treatment she always received from New Mama.

By the time Elsie was thirteen she had to make her bed and the beds of all the younger children upstairs. Then she had to be sure the floor was tidy and clean, and all clothes and other items had been picked up before she could go downstairs to help get breakfast. After breakfast she had to help clean up the table, put things away and wash all the dishes, including the big oatmeal kettle. Everything had to be clean according to New Mama's desires and THEN she could leave for school. Since the school was on the corner of their property, it was just across the back yard and through the hedgerow to get there. But it was hard for her to get there on time. It was especially hard when they had all the extra hired men to feed, and that large oatmeal kettle to clean.

School started at 8:00 a.m. and the teacher rang the school bell promptly at 8:00. Elsie loved school, she wanted to be on time and oh, how she hurried trying to get everything done so she could be there on time. She had another reason for trying so hard to be on time. If the teacher rang the 8:00 bell and Elsie was not there, then she would get a beating when she got home at noon because New Mama said she was late to school because she had dallied too long in getting her work done. What 13-year-old child could get all that work done and still be on time for school?

The teacher had eyes; she knew some harsh things were going on. She saw how Elsie and Melvina were dressed; she had also noticed some of the bruises. She knew some of the neighbors had talked to New Mama about the way she treated the children. The teacher felt sorry for Elsie so she would sometimes turn the clock back a few minutes so that she could ring the bell late and Elsie would still be in school by the time the bell rang. New Mama soon caught on to this and she began to watch the clock on her own wall at home. Then even though Elsie was in school by the time the bell rang, New Mama would say, "Aha! You were late to school again this morning you lazy thing. I was watching the clock. You cannot fool me." And Elsie would get another beating even though she had been in school by the time the teacher rang the school bell. It felt to Elsie like she was an animal caught in a trap. Trying harder or getting help from others only made matters worse. Each day she felt more dejected and discouraged and wondered if this cruel treatment would ever end.

When Elsie got a bit older, she was also taught to milk the cows which she then had to do quite regularly. Until she died, she had a very hard grip in her fingers. This came from her cow-milking days. Elsie's help was really valuable on the farm.

Soon she would finish eighth grade, the highest grade taught at the little country school on the corner of their property. Oh, how she wanted to go to school some more. New Mama said, "You are too stupid to go to school. You are so dumb and ugly no one would ever want to marry you.

It is your duty to help take care of us. The only thing you are good for is to stay on the farm and work." To be sure, Elsie did not look too good, New Mama kept her hair cut in that ugly bowl cut, and she kept Elsie's dresses so short that those ugly bloomers hung out the bottom. This was excruciatingly humiliating for a fifteen-year-old girl.

New Mama's children could go to school all they wanted, they could read, even at home, whenever they felt like it. They had music lessons whenever they wanted and enjoyed all kinds of fun engaging activities and pastimes. This just did not seem fair to Elsie, and she often wondered what she had done to make New Mama so angry towards her, Melvina, and Archie.

Something else changed on the farm. Mama and Papa had always been honest and returned a full tithe to God and had given offerings freely to all the needs presented. In return for their honoring God, he had blessed them generously. Sometime during the earlier years, New Mama decided that all this giving was not necessary. They could not afford to give a whole ten percent of all their earnings to the church. Offerings were given as the mood suited. But something strange happened, they began to have problems. Soon they had to borrow money for this or that. The house badly needed painting but they could not afford it. Even the once lovely house began to look sad and neglected. However, there always seemed to be enough money to give New Mama's children whatever they desired.

A long time after Elsie had grown up and had lived away from the farm for many years, Papa died. At that time the farm that he had built with such love, had to be sold in order to pay off all the debts that had been acquired over the hard years.

Chapter Three

The summer Elsie was sixteen, something interesting happened. Elsie was busy with her normal chores when a car drove into the driveway and right up to the back of the house. This was not a normal occurrence and certainly not on a workday in the middle of the week. Everyone was interested in the visitors, then a man and a lady got out of the car. Elsie immediately recognized them and knew it was her Grandpa Daniel and Grandma Carolina. It was always nice to see them for they were her dear Mama's mother and father and were always so very kind and loving. But what could they want? They were not frequent visitors to the farm.

About the same time that Mama and Papa had gotten married, Grandma and Grandpa had a surprise. They themselves had another little girl whom they named Maggie. So, Elsie now had two aunties and one of them was just one year older than she was. Grandpa no longer had to farm and since Lydia was married and their boys were also married and had established good farms for themselves, Grandpa Daniel and Grandma Carolina decided to move to a small city close to a boarding school so that when Maggie reached school age, she and her sister could walk to school every day. She would never have to leave home to go to a Christian boarding school.

By the time Elsie was sixteen, Grandpa Daniel and Grandma Carolina still lived in that city several hours away. That is why it was such a special treat to see them. Soon the reason for their visit was discovered. New Mama had marched right out and wanted to know what they were doing there on her farm and what they wanted.

Grandpa and Grandma said, "We have come to take Elsie to school. She is fast becoming a young lady and she needs to be in school and get as much education as she can. We will take her home with us, and she will live with us, and she can attend school at the boarding school that is near our house. She can work on the farm there to help pay her school bills, she can easily walk to and from school with our Maggie every day."

Elsie could hardly believe her ears! She was to have an opportunity to live with her loving Grandpa and Grandma, she could go to school. What could be better?

Her big hopes were soon dashed for New Mama exclaimed, "You are definitely NOT going to take her! She is too dumb and stupid to go to school and see how ugly she is. Furthermore, we need her to stay and work on the farm. Save that opportunity for someone more deserving, smart, and good looking. She is not worth the effort; she needs to stay here and help us."

"Elsie is not dumb or stupid and neither is she ugly! If she had proper clothes like the other girls her age, and her hair were allowed to grow to a reasonable length she would be a lovely young lady. It is all settled. She IS coming with us. We ARE taking her with us today!"

And so, the conversation went on for some time, but Grandpa and Grandma would not back down in their fight for Elsie. They finally won the argument with New Mama and told Elsie to get her few things and come with them. And that is just what Elsie did. New Mama was most unhappy, and she let everyone know it. She told everyone that Grandpa and Grandma had just come onto her property and kidnapped Elsie.

Elsie could hardly believe her good fortune. She knew God was watching over her. She knew her whole life would be changed, and she was so incredibly happy she could hardly wait to get to her new home. There was a special treat waiting for her there.

Grandpa and Grandma told Elsie she would share Maggie's bedroom. The girls could walk to school together every day. Grandma would make a few dresses for Elsie just like the other girls wore, she even made a special pretty dress she could wear for church and other special occasions. She could let her hair grow long, no more bowl cuts, and her grandparents treated her just like their own daughter. Grandpa and Grandma were not rich in money, but they were rich in love and happiness, and so generous with the things they did have.

Soon Elsie was settled into Maggie's bedroom. Oh, what fun! The two girls laughed and talked, and it just seemed like they were really sisters. Maggie and Elsie did everything together. Elsie did not know that life could be so happy and fun. Grandma did make her some dresses just like other girls her age wore, and her hair grew long and thick and she could tie it up in a pretty bow. Her sprinkling of freckles disappeared, and she no longer heard anyone telling her that she was an ugly old turkey egg or stupid. No one criticized Elsie for everything she did, rather she was encouraged and praised. She was loved again like her dear Mama had loved her. For the first time that she could really remember she felt so incredibly happy.

Soon Grandpa took her over to the school to meet the principal and the farm manager. There he made all the arrangements for Elsie to begin classes in the fall with all the other students. During the same visit to the school, he also arranged that she could start work immediately in the gardens of the school farm so that she could start earning some money for her books and tuition. Elsie enjoyed being outside and she certainly knew how to work in a garden and work hard. She was so glad to have work. And they were even going to pay her for the same kind of work she had done for years for which she had earned nothing but scoldings, harsh words and beatings. She was so excited because they told her that her wages would be eight whole cents an hour! She felt truly rich and very blessed. There were several other little odd jobs that Elsie was allowed to do to help her earn money toward her school bills.

Fall arrived and school started, and Elsie enjoyed going to class and being with other young people her age and Grandma and Grandpa were always so kind to her. They always treated her as their very own daughter. She could see why her own Mama had been such a kind and good person. She still missed her own Mama, but she truly loved living with her grandparents, it was like her own home and Maggie was just like her real sister. Everyday Elsie also helped her grandmother around the house.

From the time that Elsie left the farm when she was sixteen years old, she did not go back to live on the farm, but she lived with her grandparents year around.

With Elsie gone, Melvina had to take the brunt of the beatings and the harsh words from New Mama which had mostly been directed at Elsie. Both Melvina and Archie married and left the farm as soon as they possibly could. Archie was really too young to make such an important decision, but he just could not stay in that place any longer. One particularly good thing happened when Melvina married and left the farm. She was able to get Mama's and Papa's two wedding portraits from the dining room wall and take them with her. Now they were totally safe from New Mama's destruction. Today those 2 pictures hang on the wall in the home of Carol, Elsie's oldest daughter.

During the summer she worked long days and even during the school year, she worked as much as possible to help pay her tuition. Elsie worked hard on her classes, and she worked hard on the farm, picking peas, beans, tomatoes, carrots, or whatever crop needed to be harvested. During the winter when there were no vegetables to pick, she was able to do other odd jobs, like cleaning and helping to grade papers. She was so thankful for the work and the pay she received.

During the summer it would get so hot working in the garden, which was really tiring work. There were several other young ladies picking produce from the garden as she did. They were all chattering as they worked, and the other girls would pause and stand up and stretch to relax their muscles every now and then, but Elsie just kept on working. She was simply too shy to do much chattering with the others and she had learned to concentrate on working hard, even when it was uncomfortable and was so tired.

One day while they were picking vegetables, someone came out to the garden and called, "Elsie, the principal wants to see you." What a fright! Being called in to see the principal could only mean one thing. She was in trouble. It seemed like her heart was going to jump right out of her mouth. She thought and thought but could not think of anything she had done wrong. She had known only scolding, harsh words, and punishment for the work she had done. Her feet felt so very heavy, and she wondered if she could make it all the way to his office. All the way there, she worried. What was to become of her now? She had a big lump of scare in her throat.

When she timidly knocked on the door, she heard a cheerful, "come in." She did and then the principal said, "Elsie, I have been watching you work."

Oh dear, what had she done not quite well enough? But then he continued, "look out that window." Trying to keep her tears from coming, Elsie turned to look out the window as he had asked her to do. The principal quizzed her, "Now tell me: What do you see?" She said, "I see the gardens and the other girls working."

"Yes," answered the principal. "I, also, can see them all working. For quite some time now I have been watching you all work.

Her mind was racing, what could be the matter with her work? What was he going to say? Then before she could say anything else he continued.

"What I have seen is everyone talking and chattering. They take breaks and stand and stretch and look around. That is, everyone except you. You just keep on working and working and do not take any breaks. You are a very industrious worker. I appreciate the excellent work you are doing. I know your salary is eight cents an hour, but I am going to raise your pay to ten cents an hour from now on."

Elsie was overjoyed. A raise! Ten cents an hour! And he had praised her work. She was not accustomed to praise like this. She went back to the garden with a happy mind and a song in her heart.

The weeks and months seemed to fly by. Elsie liked her classes. She enjoyed her new friends. She loved having Maggie for her sister and Grandma and Grandpa were always so kind and loving to her. It seemed that before she realized it, graduation time was just around the corner. Elsie would be graduating from high school. For graduation Grandma made Elsie a special new dress, just like she had done for Maggie.

Graduation time came. Elsie would have loved to see Papa, but New Mama said he was too busy on the farm and could not come for such a frivolous thing. So, Elsie graduated without her father or her brother or sister, but she had Maggie, Grandma and Grandpa. They were so proud of her and loved her so much.

There was a junior college on the same campus as the high school and Grandma and Grandpa encouraged her to stay in school and continue her education. New Mama thought she should come back to the farm and work, but Elsie was with Grandma and Grandpa now and she happily followed their advice. In the summer she continued to work on the school farm.

In the fall, she started college. Things went along pretty much as they had been but after some time, she noticed that a certain young man seemed to be watching her. He was a very diligent worker and had to work as hard as she did to help pay for his school tuition and books. So, they did not have that much time to get to know each other. However, when young people take an interest in one another, they somehow seem to find a few minutes here and there to get acquainted.

New Mama had told her that she was so ugly no one would look at her and no one would ever want her as a wife. Yet it seemed that this young man saw her with different eyes than New Mama had seen her. He looked at her as if she were beautiful. And he made her feel like she was worth spending his whole life with her. And that is the way it happened with Elsie and Lloyd, for that was his name.

Since both Elsie and Lloyd had to work such long hours, they did not have much time to socialize and do fun things as did many of the other students. In the winter, they did get to go ice skating sometimes and that was such fun.

Lloyd was always polite and considerate of Elsie. Every now and then he had an opportunity to walk her home from school. Elsie explained to him that she lived with her grandparents, and she introduced him to her grandpa and grandma. They were quite impressed with the type of young man he was. He also told Elsie that he wanted to become a pastor just like his dad was. Lloyd certainly admired his father!

As Elsie and Lloyd got to know each other better she began to trust him enough to tell him a bit about her past and some of the things that had happened to her as she was growing up. He could certainly understand why she lived with Grandpa Daniel and Grandma Carolina and Lloyd was glad they had rescued her from the life she had suffered on the farm. He also shared with her some of his own experiences growing up as a pastor's son.

Chapter Four

Ever since he could remember his dad had been a pastor and one of Lloyd's early memories was of going to camp meeting with his parents. Dad would have to go early to help set up all the tents. Then Mother, Dad, and Lloyd would stay all through camp meeting and afterwards their family stayed at the campground while Dad helped take down all the tents and store them for the next year.

Of course, this was a lot of work and being gone from home for such a long time took a lot of preparation. Mother had to prepare for being away from home for several weeks. That involved doing cooking, baking, and canning enough food to last the three of them for the whole time they were gone. She washed the clothes the family would need and mended the ones that needed mending. It also involved taking bedding and housekeeping items so she could properly care for her family while they were at camp meeting because the family would live in one of the tents the same as did the other families who spent the whole time at camp. It was a lot of work but finally it was all ready.

When it was time to go, Dad packed their car. The cars in the early 1920's were not like the cars we have today, their car was small and had no trunk in which to pack things. In went Dad's books, the kettles, the clothes, the bedding, the food, the pillows, and everything the whole family would need for ten days of camp meeting plus the weeks before setting up the tents, and the weeks afterwards taking them down and putting them all away. There were boxes and bags everywhere; on the floor, the seats, Dad even tied boxes to the running boards, and Mother had bags on the floor between her feet. On top of it all went the bedding. There was just enough room for Dad to sit and drive, Mother sat up front, and the only place for Lloyd was lying flat on his tummy on top of the bedding. He was young and fit just fine and he could look out the front window and see where they were going. It was quite an adventure for him.

Not only were the cars in the early 1920's different than the cars we have today, the roads were also very different. Sometimes they just rode across the prairie, and when they came to a hill, Dad would have to turn around and back up the hill. The gas tank was in the back of the car and if the front end of the car was higher than the back end, the gasoline would run out of the tank. Sometimes they had dirt roads. If it were dry the roads would be so dusty. If it were raining the roads would be very muddy. Often the road became thick with heavy mud which was called "gumbo." This would stick to the tires and Dad would have to get out and scrape it from the tires so their tires could continue to go round and round, and the family could go on with their journey.

On this trip it started to rain, first a little, then great big drops, and then it really poured, and the road became very muddy. Dad came to a small hill, and he had to steer so very carefully but the car slowly climbed the hill and then started slipping and sliding down the other side. At the bottom of the hill there was quite a sharp turn towards the left, and across a narrow bridge, and then the road continued its way on the other side of the river. The three of them could see a couple of cars on the other side of the narrow bridge waiting for their turn to cross because the bridge had only one lane, so cars could cross the bridge going only one way at a time. Dad held tightly onto the steering wheel and slowly started down the slippery, muddy road. The people could see the car sliding down the hill and did not want to be hit by a sliding car. It was best to sit and wait than to be hit by a car which was sliding out of control.

Even though Dad held on to the steering wheel as tightly as he could, he soon realized that he would not be able to control the car so that they could safely make the left turn at the bottom of the hill. Mother and Dad realized that their car was going to roll over and maybe even go into the river. The family said a quick prayer to God for help as the car continued to slip and slide down the hill because it was so slippery that Dad knew he could not stop the car. Then, just as they got to the turn, the whole car was picked up, floated on the air across the river, and then set gently down in the deep grass on the other side. Mother, Dad, and Lloyd never even felt a bump because the car was set down so gently. Mother and Dad right away said a quick thank you to God for His love, care, and special protection of their family.

The people who had been waiting to cross the bridge jumped out of their cars and came running down to where the car sat. "We saw that! We saw what happened! It looked like someone just carried your car across the river and gently set it down on this side." Their faces were pale, and the people said no one could understand what they had just seen. Then the strongest men began to try to push the car up onto the road, but it would not move. Dad went walking down the road to the nearest farm to ask for help. The farmer gladly brought his tractor but even the tractor could not move the car. The mud was so heavy and so slippery that the tractor wheels just spun around and around but would not move. Then the farmer went back home and brought his strongest and best work horses, and these horses were able to pull the car up onto the road again. Mother, Dad, and Lloyd gladly and safely went on their way to camp meeting.

Dad was not only a preacher he was also an evangelist. He would go from town to town, put up a large tent and hold meetings to tell the people of Jesus' great love for them and explain what the Bible really teaches. Many of the people chose to love and follow Jesus, by doing what they had learned from the Bible.

Lloyd had so many experiences to tell Elsie that she was beginning to see why he had such a powerful desire to become a preacher like his dad. She began to admire him even more.

Usually when Dad would pitch his big tent where he was to hold the meetings, he would also put up a smaller tent behind the big one and Mother, Dad, and Lloyd would live in the small tent while the meetings were being held. This was convenient because Mother and Lloyd could help him keep an eye on the things in the tents, especially during the day when there were no meetings.

Many times, after a few meetings were held, some of the town's other ministers became angry that their parishioners were happily attending the meetings. Dad was very careful to use only the Bible when he preached, and he always allowed the people time to find the texts which he used in their own Bibles and read for themselves what the Bible taught.

Dad loved God so much and He always emphasized how much God loved the people and how God wants them to be with Him in heaven for ever and ever. He did not scare the people about burning in hell forever so that they would obey God. He said people are to obey God out of love. He also told them that the Bible teaches people can pray directly to God, talk to Him as their Friend. No one needs to have any other human mediator God is their personal Friend. Dad also explained that no one needs to do any penances to have their sins forgiven. No kneeling for hours on end, no special and costly journeys, nor paying large sums to the church or church leaders to have their sins forgiven. Just ask God and because of His great love for us, He is so willing and happy to forgive when people ask Him to forgive them.

Often when the listeners learned something which was new to them, these parishioners would go to their own pastors and ask their pastor about what they had heard and learned in the meeting. This was particularly true when Dad told the people about the seventh-day Sabbath. Most people had never heard that the Bible teaches people to worship on the seventh day. But Dad was incredibly careful to show them from the Bible that God created the world in six days and blessed the seventh day and rested on it. Because He created everything in six days, He made this special day for people to pause their daily work, and rest and spend this day with Him, thinking about all the things He has done for them, and worshipping Him. Because that is the day He rested and blessed, He gave His people the privilege of having a special day just to rest and worship Him on that same day. We are to do all our work in six days and then stop our work and worship God on the seventh day for that is the only day He has blessed as special.

When people asked their pastors about keeping the seventh-day Sabbath holy, the pastors could not give them an answer from the Bible so they would say something like, "well, tradition teaches us differently." Or "we have always followed our traditions and there is no need to change now." Or "most of the world cannot be wrong and only a few people right." These pastors felt their congregations would be diminished when people started to follow what the Bible says and begin to worship God on His holy seventh day.

Other ministers were not the only ones who got angry. Sometimes the people who attended the meetings would become angry. Many were farmers and had to work hard all year, especially during planting and harvesting times. Farmers had to get the crops planted and then later harvested before damaging rains came. In one town there was a certain family who came to the meetings every night and were really enjoying what they were hearing about God. Not only the mother and father, but all their children, came faithfully, every evening. Then one night Dad talked about the Bible Sabbath and how God wants us to honor Him by keeping the seventh day holy. This really bothered Farmer Jones, he thought he needed to work seven days a week to get all his farming done. He was noticeably quiet on the way home that night. When he got home, he told his wife, "We are not going to those meetings anymore." The wife and children were very disappointed, but father's word was law. Therefore, the next night no one from this family attended the meeting.

Now, Dad was not just a preacher and an evangelist, he genuinely loved people and he wanted to share God's love with as many people as he could. He would preach at night and during the day he would go around and visit the people who had come to the meetings. When the Jones family did not attend one night, Dad was concerned. The next day he went out to visit them at their home to make sure there was nothing the matter. Yes, the family was just fine, but simply were not interested in coming any more. Dad could tell that Mrs. Jones did not agree with her husband but he did not want to interfere with their family affairs.

Farmer Jones was coolly polite while Dad was there but inside, he was truly angry that Dad had come to their farm to visit them. In fact, he was so angry that after Dad left, he told his wife, "If that preacher man ever comes out here again and ever sets foot on my land, I am going to run the pitchfork right through him." His wife knew this was no idle threat and she wondered what would happen if the preacher did come again.

Dad was totally unaware of this threat so after missing the Jones family for a couple more nights, Dad decided to go out and visit them again to see if he could encourage them. This family loved Jesus and had all been so extremely interested in the truths they were learning right from their Bibles. So, one morning, Dad went out to their farm. As he got near the farmhouse, he could see Farmer Jones was out in the field as it was haying time. Dad, being the friendly, helpful person that he was, stopped and walked across the field and in a friendly manner greeted the farmer. He then said, "I see you are pitching hay, if you'll give me an extra pitchfork, I'll help you load your wagon."

The farmer was speechless, no one had ever offered to help him for free before and what frugal, hard-working farmer is going to turn down free help. He was too shocked to do anything but give Dad an extra pitchfork. Soon Dad had a pitchfork and was pitching hay as fast and well as Farmer Jones. Farmer Jones did not know that Dad had been a farmer before he was a preacher, so Dad really knew how to work hard and well. All morning they worked side by side, as they worked, they chatted and laughed together. Dad had a real sense of humor and he liked to laugh and tell jokes. He never once mentioned the meetings or anything religious. They just worked hard, chatted, laughed, and got a lot of work done.

At noon time Dad prepared to leave and go home but Farmer Jones said, "No come to the house and have dinner with us. The wife always prepares a lot of good food." Then, he and Dad went towards the house. When Mrs. Farmer looked out the window and saw her husband and the preacher come walking towards the house, she did not know what to think. Was she going to witness a murder before her very eyes? Her husband had been so positive about destroying the preacher and she knew he meant what he said. When they came into the house Farmer Jones said, "Wife put on an extra plate. The preacher man is going to eat dinner with us."

That is one request she was most happy to fulfill, and they had a good hearty meal and then Dad told them he had to go back to prepare for the evening service. Then he just bid them goodbye. But still he did not mention anything religious or the fact that no one from their family had been to the meetings lately.

That night Farmer Jones, along with his wife and children were all at the meetings and they never missed another one. Farmer Jones soon learned that when he took time to honor God and do what God required of him, God blessed in a double way, and he could get more done in six days of work than he used to in seven days, while he and his family all worshiped God on His holy seventh day.

Dad's friendliness and helpfulness brought many people to know the truth of God's great love, and out of that love to obey God's commandments to show their love for Him.

Lloyd loved to help his dad with the meetings which he held, and he had a powerful desire to follow in his dad's footsteps. Usually, Dad pitched the large tent and Mother, Dad, and Lloyd lived in the small tent behind it, but occasionally Dad was fortunate enough to find a room or part of a basement which he could rent, and the family appreciated living in a "real" house for a change.

In one town Dad did find a part of a house to rent. So, every night after the meeting Mother and Lloyd would pick up the song books and straighten things out while Dad put things away for the night. Then he would put down all the tent flaps and tie them securely and the three of them would walk to the home where they were staying. Since it was always dark, and everyone was tired after a long day's work Dad figured out which was the shortest and quickest way to walk home. The family took the same route every night and all of them enjoyed the quiet and peace of the late-night walk.

One night it was a particularly lovely evening and after everything had been put away and tied down well, the three of them started home, but Dad suddenly said, "This is such an especially lovely night, let's walk a different way tonight." And so, they did.

The next morning while Dad was running some errands in town, one of the men from town met him and asked. "Hey, preacher man, why didn't you go home last night?"

Dad answered, "Oh, we did!" "No, you didn't." "Yes, we did. Why do you ask?" Then the man told Dad this story.

There a few of the preachers in town who do not want you here and they want to get rid of you, so this group of preachers hired some of us men to kill you and your family when you were on your way home last night. We knew you always left the tent after the meeting and always took the same route home. At a certain corner where you always passed, we were hiding behind a building and waiting to jump out and attack you when you came by. We waited and waited a long time after you usually go home, but you never came last night. Eventually we gave up and went home. "So why didn't you go home last night?"

Then Dad told him that all three of them had gone home, but because it was such a lovely evening, had chosen to walk home by a different way that evening.

Dad had many experiences in which he could see God's hand protecting him and saving his life. Many were very serious, some were quite frightening, but some instances were just plain funny.

Dad loved the people, and he loved to visit them and most of his mornings were spent visiting and then the afternoons he would prepare for his meetings. Often when he came to a new area, he would spend several days visiting the people and getting to know them before the meetings started. He had many long days like that and when he was quite a distance from home, he would have to find a place to spend the night. There were not so many hotels, and even when there was one, he usually could not afford it so he would find a family who seemed friendly and would just ask if he could sleep there that night. Sometimes the family would see that it was already late in the afternoon and would offer him a place to sleep.

But not everyone was friendly, sometimes people sent their dogs to chase him away, sometimes the people just hollered at him to leave their property, other times some of them grudgingly allowed him to stay for the night. With his sense of humor, he told us that when he came to a home that seemed receptive, he would say he used to ask "lady (or sir), could I please have a drink of water? I'm so hungry I don't know where I'm going to sleep tonight." Whether he really said it or not, we do not know but he did have a great sense of humor and that sounds like something he would say, and he did have many interesting experiences.

One afternoon, towards evening he came to a farm way out in the country, all by itself. When he talked to the people, he could tell they were not really welcoming, especially not the husband, but they were not openly hostile. He had met quite a few hostile people in that area, so he wanted to find a place to spend the night before it got too late. Finally, he just asked whether they had an extra bed which he could use just for that night. They told him, "No, but you can have the room at the back of the house where our daughters sleep, and they will sleep elsewhere for this night." Dad very willingly and gratefully accepted their offer and after the evening meal he prepared to retire for the night. It was dark and the wife lit a lamp for him to use and he bid the family good night then he went to the room he had been assigned and prepared for bed. He was so tired he blew out the lantern and went to bed. He had not been asleep too long when he heard his bedroom door slowly open. With the receptions he had received in the area, he wondered what was coming next, but decided that the best thing to do was to lie still and pretend to be asleep.

He opened one eye just a slit to see what he could see, but he laid perfectly still. The door opened slowly and soon it was open just enough to let the man of the house slip into his room. By the light that came in from the hall, Dad could see that in the man's right hand was a huge butcher knife, and the man slowly and carefully tip-toed across the room until he was right beside the bed by Dad's head.

Should Dad scream, pretend to be asleep, should he jump at the man, or what? So, he decided the best thing to do would be to just lie very still but be alert and watch the man out of the slit in his eye. Let the man make the first move.

When the man was right by Dad's head, he slowly raised that big butcher knife, up, up, and up a little bit more. Then with his left hand he reached up and grabbed something and began to slice. He sliced off a nice big chunk of salami, then slowly and quietly turned and tip-toed out of the room and shut the door. Dad had been so tired when he went to bed that he had not even noticed there were several large salamis hanging from the rafters up near the ceiling, just over the bed. The man had just wanted a late-night snack!

Elsie always loved to hear Lloyd tell the experiences that he and his parents had had as they went to different towns. She loved hearing about the people, about how much Lloyd's mother and dad loved the people and how much they helped people. She knew that when she met his parents, she would love them. And she did! Lloyd's parents were so kind to her and treated her just like their own daughter. Lloyd's home had been so vastly different than hers had been. Would she ever be privileged to become part of a family like that? For now, they were both remarkably busy with school. But there were brief times when they had time together and Lloyd could tell her about his family.

Sometimes the people who had been coming to the meetings were so happy about the good news they were hearing that they really became very friendly with Mother and Dad. One such family invited them to come over for dinner and of course Mother and Dad accepted. After the meal, the lady of the house brought out a delicious pie for dessert. Oh, it was so good, and Dad praised her for it. Then she asked, "Preacher man, will you have another piece?" Dad was so full that he said, "Oh, no, I couldn't possibly eat another bite. It was all so good I really ate my fill but thank you anyway."

The lady was quite insistent and after Dad had refused several times, he began to wonder if it would hurt her feelings if he did not go ahead and take the offered extra piece so he told her that he would be glad to have another piece even though he was very full already.

Then the lady said, "Oh, preacher man, I am so sorry. I do not have any more pie. I was just trying to be hospitable."

Seems like it is best to always be totally honest.

By the summer Lloyd was fourteen Mother and Dad had had another baby boy. There were thirteen years difference in the boys' ages. But Lloyd loved his baby brother, even though he did not get to know him very well because by then Lloyd would often go and work for other farmers during the day just to help earn a bit of cash.

That summer Dad pitched their small tent behind the large tent again. During the day Lloyd would go and help some of the farmers. At night he would come to the tent and help to baby-sit for his baby brother. Mother had a lovely voice, and she would often sing special music for Dad's meetings. She also liked to stand at the entrance and greet the people as they came in for the service. Lloyd's help was much appreciated every evening as he helped to care for his baby brother and handed out song books.

As happened in some other places, one of the other preachers in town was not happy that some of the members of his congregation were attending the meetings and enjoying hearing and learning the Biblical truths. He tried to talk against Dad when he preached in his church and whenever he got the chance to talk with his parishioners. He thought he was going to lose some of his members to this "7-days preacher." Dad would never argue with either the other preachers or with the people, but he always had Bible texts to prove anything he said and of course the people liked being able to see and read the answers to their questions in their own Bibles.

Dad was always so helpful, and he did have a small car so when one of the townsmen said he needed help in getting to a nearby town so he could go to the doctor the next day and wondered if Dad would drive him there, Dad happily agreed. Mother would accompany him and they were to leave at 5:00 a.m. the next morning. Since roads were unpredictable at best and cars did not go as fast as they do today, Dad knew it would be a long and exhausting day. He needed to get the man to the other town, and accomplish everything that needed to be done, and then return that same day and be ready for the evening meeting. Even though he knew it would be hard he thought he could do it and he agreed to take the man.

Dad told Lloyd, "Mother and I are going to leave while it is still dark, but you will be in charge while I am gone. Please take good care of everything." Lloyd was a very responsible fourteen-year-old and Dad had confidence that everything would be well taken care of with Lloyd in charge.

That night Dad preached the sermon as usual but afterwards he did not feel comfortable. He felt that something was not quite right. After the meeting had finished that night, Mother, Dad, and Lloyd cleaned up as usual and made sure everything was closed and safe and then they went to their small tent to prepare for bed for the night. Lloyd went to bed and to sleep, so did baby brother, but Dad and Mother stayed up. All night long the two of them walked around the outside of the tents. Mother and Dad walked until 2:00 a.m. and finally went to bed. At 5:00 a.m. it was still dark, but Mother and Dad got up, dressed and went to the car and left to go pick up the man he had promised to take to the doctor in the next town.

Lloyd was still sound asleep, but suddenly, even though it was still dark, he woke up and could not go back to sleep. He knew he had a lot of responsibility and he kept thinking of everything that was now his responsibility. So, he got up and went outside to look at the big tent.

The big tent had three very large poles going front to back down the center of the tent. These supported all the weight for that big tent. It was a lot of weight and very heavy. Around the sides, there were more poles, somewhat smaller to help hold up the sides and the tent flaps. Lloyd decided to walk around the tent just to be sure that everything was closed tightly and safe. As he walked, he pulled on each rope to check its tightness. The tight tension of the ropes helped to keep the tent in position and safe.

He put his hand on one of the main ropes and gave it a tug. The rope came loose in his hand. That was certainly a strange thing to happen! It should have been tightly tied to the stake in the ground beside that pole. When he bent down to examine it more closely, he saw that someone had cut completely through the rope! He loosened it from the stake and took both ends and tied a strong knot in it so that it was whole again then he tied it tightly to the stake.

He walked on to the next pole and there again he found that the rope had been cut completely in two, just like the other rope. Again, he made a strong knot with the two ends and re-tied the rope tightly to the stake. He went to the next rope, and it was the same thing. This had been done deliberately! He went all around the big tent and found every rope on two of the sides had been cut completely through. He worked as fast and hard as he could, finishing just as it began to get light. Then he walked around the tent again and pulled on each rope to be sure all were snug and tight and properly tied to their stakes. Just as he finished and walked into the little family tent, a strong wind came up. It blew and blew and turned into a hard summer storm with lots of extraordinarily strong winds and rain. The large tent was stable and stood fast.

When Dad came home late that afternoon, he saw all the large knots and asked, "What happened here?" Lloyd told Dad how he could not sleep and when he got up to check he found all the ropes had been cut on two sides of the big tent so he tied them with strong knots as best as he could. Dad was so proud of the good work that Lloyd had done. Then Dad told Lloyd what should have happened. Whoever cut the ropes, had cut them all on the far side away from their small tent and cut them in such a manner that if even a slight wind had come up, it would have blown down the big tent; and the huge poles in the middle of that big tent would have fallen right across the small tent in which the family was sleeping and all of them would have been killed instantly.

As soon as possible, Dad and Lloyd went to one rope at a time, untied it, spliced it strongly, and then retied it to its stake until all were safely and firmly tied again. It was strong and looked neat again, not messy like the big temporary knots had looked. When the people found out what had happened some of them asked Dad if they should go and call the police and tell the police what had been done. Dad said, "No, we'll just wait let God take care of us." Many times, God put His protecting hand over them and took care of them. But none of them ever found out what had happened in New Leipsig, North Dakota that summer.

Fifteen years later Lloyd and his family were visiting his Uncle Jake in North Dakota when Uncle Jake suddenly asked, "Lloyd did your dad ever hold meetings in New Leipsig in such and such a year?"

Lloyd answered that yes, he had, and wondered why Uncle Jake asked that question. Here is the answer Uncle Jake gave Lloyd. Uncle Jake had been to camp meeting that summer and one of the men on the campground, recognizing his last name, had come up to him and asked if Uncle Jake had ever held meetings in New Leipsig. "Oh, no! I am a farmer. But my brother, Sam is a preacher and I'm sure he did." Then that man told Uncle Jake the following story.

In such and such a year a preacher man came to our town and put up a big tent and held meetings. That preacher man and his family lived in a small tent at the back of the big tent. One of the other ministers in town was not happy that so many people, even from his church, were attending those meetings and the disgruntled minister paid me to kill the visiting preacher man. We decided the easiest way to accomplish that fact was to make it look like their deaths had been an accident and we decided on a plane of action.

We knew that a heavy storm was forecasted for a certain night. Therefore, after the meeting that night, I drove to a nearby hill and sat in my car to watch the tent and the Preacher man's family. As soon as the meeting was over, and all the people had gone home, when everything was quiet, and the preacher man and his family had gone to bed, I was going to go and cut all the ropes on the big tent. However, I was to cut only the ropes on the two sides farthest away from the family tent. When the slightest breeze came up it would cause the big tent and poles to fall on the small family tent and the preacher man and his family would all be killed by the large center poles falling on them while they were asleep in their tent. With the large storm predicted for that night we were sure this plan looking like ad accident when fulfilled, would be a success and we need not worry about that preacher man anymore.

I sat in my car on the hill in the dark and waited and watched. All the people had gone home, the big tent was closed down and all the tent flaps well tied and then something strange happened. The preacher man and his wife did not go to bed. All night long they walked around and around and around the large tent. They continued walking until 2:00 a.m. and finally they went to bed. As quickly and as quietly as I could, I immediately went down to the tent and cut all the ropes on the two sides opposite the small family tent. That way the slightest breeze would bring the large center poles and big tent down right across their small family tent. Then I returned to my car and waited and watched for it to happen. But no storm, not even a small wind, came up and at 5:00 a.m. the preacher man came out to his car and drove away.

The preacher man had no sooner left than his son came out and started to check the ropes on the large tent. Immediately he discovered that I had cut the main ropes, and he started to tie the ropes together! As soon as he was done and went back to the family tent, the predicted strong wind and storm came up, but the large tent stood safely.

So, the mystery of who cut the ropes was solved many years later. But during those years, someone who was paid to commit murder, gave his heart to the Lord! God is so very good, and He loves us so very much!

The weeks and months were going by so fast. Soon it would be graduation time again. Elsie knew that Lloyd would have to go away to a senior college so that he could finish his degree and he could become a minister like Samuel, his dad. What would happen when Lloyd left? What would Elsie do? Would he go away and forget all about her?

Shortly before graduation, the school had a picnic in a nearby national park. It was such a beautiful place, mountains, rivers, waterfalls. It was such a peaceful and gorgeous place, just the kind of place to go for a relaxing day before final exams. At last, a day when both Elsie and Lloyd could enjoy relaxing together and doing something fun instead of just work and study all the time. They took advantage of this day to spend a little time together. They were walking along a path that ran alongside one of the rivers and came to a lovely waterfall. They just stood there a few minutes enjoying the sound of the water rushing over the falls and the peacefulness of the whole scene.

Suddenly Lloyd turned and said, "Elsie, would you be willing to darn my socks for the rest of your life?" He must have inherited his dad's sense of humor because that was quite a way to propose. She was happy to say, "yes." She knew she would be a part of a happy, loving family who not only loved each other but also loved and served God. She knew Grandpa Daniel and Grandma Carolina both loved Lloyd and thought very highly of him. They had invited him to their home many times and were quite well acquainted with him by this time. Elsie had met Lloyd's parents and loved them very much. They were both loving and kind to her. Elsie knew that after she and Lloyd were married His mother, Lydia, would become the Mama she had lost when she was a little girl.

But there was a problem. Lloyd had to go away to a senior college to finish his degree so that he could fulfil his goal and become a minister. Elsie knew she could not do that. She had no money and New Mama, and Papa certainly would not help her at all. New Mama expected that Elsie would return to the farm and pick up all her work which she had left when Grandpa and Grandma had taken her away to go to school. New Mama was anxious to have Elsie's good help on the farm again.

Elsie and Lloyd discussed this problem with Grandpa and Grandma and both of them strongly encouraged her to follow Lloyd to the senior college. Grandpa and Grandma even promised that they would help her financially as much as possible.

Both of them knew she would work hard to earn as much of her school tuition as she could. That decided the matter, and both Lloyd and Elsie would go away to the senior college.

Again, New Mama said Papa had too much work to do on the farm and could not afford to come to such an unimportant occasion as graduation from junior college. But it was a happy time anyway because Lloyd's parents, Samuel and Lydia were there, Grandma Carolina and Grandpa Daniel were there, and Lloyd and Elsie knew they would both be together at the new school.

They were so happy to be able to be close to each other. They both worked awfully hard and long hours. They did not have much time for fun and relaxing but since Lloyd was in charge of overseeing the college store and the post office, she would get to see him when she went for the mail or had an errand at the store. Here and there the two of them had little minutes to see each other and talk together.

After two years, Lloyd was approaching graduation. Elsie had had to work so much extra that she did not get all her schoolwork done so she was not able to graduate. But she was so proud of Lloyd and so happy for him. He had received a call to be a minister of several small churches in a district in far northern Canada. Lloyd and Elsie planned on getting married as soon as he graduated. Now there was a wedding to plan! The two of them decided to get married the same day that Lloyd graduated for then His Mother and Dad would be there, Grandma and Grandpa would be there as well as their college friends.

Grandpa was so pleased and proud of both Lloyd and Elsie that he gave her fifty dollars to guy the necessary things for her wedding. Just imagine that! Fifty whole dollars that she could spend just as she pleased. She was very careful in how she spent that money. She was able to buy her wedding dress, veil, cake, some flowers, and a few other small things but she felt so very blessed and fortunate.

As soon as Lloyd had graduated, they began to set things up for their wedding. They chose to have their reception in the backyard of one of the faculty members. Theirs was a lovely, but simple wedding on June 6, 1937 and what a joy to share it with Mother and Dad, Grandpa and Grandma, and their college friends. Of course, again, New Mama would not allow Papa to attend Elsie's wedding. She said they could not afford it and he had too much farm work to do. New Mama was most unhappy about this wedding, now she knew that Elsie would never return to the farm to do all the work New Mama had planned for Elsie to do.

Lloyd and Elsie had one challenging and not-so-happy surprise on the day of their wedding. There was a fire in the shop which was to provide her wedding bouquet. What should they do at the last minute and her wedding money was all used up? The faculty member who had kindly offered their yard for the reception had many large, beautiful peony bushes and the wife generously offered Elsie all the fresh pink peonies she could use. The peony, especially the pink ones were a special flower for Else for the rest of her life.

There was one big happy surprise at their wedding. Mother and Dad had found a used car and bought it for Lloyd and Elsie. It was small and black, but it would be all theirs. Their very own car! It would make it so much easier for Lloyd to visit all his churches. He could go when and where he needed to go. He did not have to go by horse, which would have been most uncomfortable in the bitter cold. He did not have to wait for a train and go only where the trains went. It would be their very own and he could use it as he needed to. Oh, what a great blessing that little car was for them.

In gratitude, Lloyd and Elsie spent their honeymoon painting a used house that was close to Dad's new church. Mother and Dad were planning to move into it as soon as it was ready for them. Even though it was challenging work, they were together, and they had an enjoyable time painting together! Lloyd and Elsie were happy to do this small task to help Mother and Dad.

Lloyd used to enjoy telling people that he got his Batchelor's degree in the morning and that afternoon Elsie took it away from him. Again, that was his sense of humor, which he inherited from his dad shining through.

New Mama was so angry that Elsie and Lloyd had married that she would not even allow Lloyd to set foot on the farm property. Lloyd and Elsie remained friendly and kept trying to come visit Papa and New Mama and, but it was quite a while until New Mama grudgingly allowed them on "her" property.

Sometime after they were married, she finally allowed them on the farm. Papa was so kind to Lloyd; he was so proud of what Elsie and Lloyd were doing and he completely accepted Lloyd. On one of these visits Lloyd decided to have a talk with Papa. Lloyd asked why Elsie, Melvina, and Archie had been so mistreated. He wanted to know why Elsie had such terrible scars on her back from all the beatings New Mama had given her.

Poor Papa, he did not know what to say. He had no idea that New Mama had been treating his precious children in this manner. He did not know about all the beatings. Maybe he was so busy with all the farm work. Then perhaps New Mama was not very kind to him either. So maybe it was a relief and an escape for him to stay away from the house as much as possible. Maybe she told him everything was going well in the home. Whatever the reason, he had been ignorant of all that went on when he was out of the house.

In those days children were expected to be seen and not heard. Also, in those days the house and children were the wife's responsibility and earning a living or taking care of the farm were the husband's responsibility. Maybe for this reason, he did not even try to find out what was happening inside his own home. One time Elsie had confided to Papa that New Mama had beaten her. Later on, when Papa was outside working New Mama scolded her and said she should keep her mouth shut and not "tell tales" to her Papa and then she had received such a whipping from New Mama that she just kept her mouth shut after that. Perhaps Papa assumed that the beatings were no longer happening. No one knows.

And no one ever knew why New Mama was so mean and cruel. When Elsie was a grown lady one of her uncles, a brother of New Mama's said, "We talked to her, we asked her to treat you children in a kindlier manner, but she would not listen to anyone."

Maybe it was because when New Mama was a young lady, a new doctor came to her town. He was single and he was a doctor. She developed a hard crush on him. She was hoping to win him and become a doctor's wife. Then Papa came along, needing a wife. He had been married to her cousin and he had a large prosperous farm. He had built her a beautiful home on that farm. Maybe her parents had thought her future was more secure if she married a well-established, successful farmer than if she would marry an unknown poor young country doctor.

Did they arrange the marriage of their daughter to Papa, did they forbid their daughter to marry the unknow young man she had fixed her eyes on? Maybe she never got over that and felt Papa's three children were responsible for robbing her of her future as a doctor's wife. For whatever reason she took out her anger on the three of them. All her life she was a very prickly person, and no one knows why.

All that was past now, and Elsie and Lloyd were starting their new life. They had a happy home but the rest of her life she suffered the effects of how she had been treated as a child. She paid a high cost for the many beatings and the constant verbal abuse she had received during her growing-up years.

Chapter Five

It was not long before Lloyd and Elsie were ready to begin their venture as minister and wife. They were assigned to a district in a far northern area of Canada. It was quite a primitive area, and the people were mostly subsistence farmers and were extremely poor. It would be quite a challenging place to work. It would also be valuable experience for a new minister. More experienced ministers had better districts. But Lloyd did not mind. He was simply happy to be a "real" minister. Now he could tell people about Jesus' great love for them and what the Bible really teaches.

They had no place to live. It was so primitive there were no houses, or apartments to rent. What should they do? Finally, the farmers in the area decided that Elsie and Lloyd could live with one of the farm families. There was one family who seemed to have a bit more space than most of the families in that area and that is the family where it was chosen for them to live.

Elsie and Lloyd were given a lean-to at one side of the house. It was not much of a home, but it did have two windows, it also had a door which they could close and lock. They were glad for that door. The lean-to was not very clean, and Elsie immediately began to scrub and clean their new home. She was a hard worker so she scrubbed as hard as she could. Lloyd put his books in a wooden packing box which was turned on its end and that became his bookcase. Elsie didn't have many dishes or kettles, so these were soon stored in another wooden box in the same way as Lloyd had stored his books. Their few clothes were stored in the same way. Soon it was "home" for them.

When it got dark, Lloyd and Elsie had a lantern which they could use to light their home. Obviously, the people were all curious to see how their new minister and wife lived and what a minister and his wife did when he was not preaching. With much curiosity the people all watched everything that Lloyd and Elsie did. People would come in and go out as they pleased so Elsie and Lloyd were exceptionally glad that their door was one which could be closed and locked. Especially when it was time to go to bed! The first night in their new place Elsie and Lloyd started to prepare for bed and when they looked up both windows were full of faces! Children's faces, mothers, fathers, grandparents, uncles, and aunts, even the neighbors came, and everyone vied for the best place and best view of how the minister and his wife were going to sleep. Did they sleep in their clothes, did they have some type of clothes to sleep in? There were so many unanswered questions.

Now Elsie and Lloyd were especially glad that their room had a door which could be closed and locked. To solve the matter of all the faces at the windows, Lloyd just turned out the lantern and the two of them prepared for bed in the dark!

The next morning when Lloyd and Elsie woke up the windows were full of faces again. Farmers are used to getting up early. The people were not rude; they were poor, lived very simply, and were just very curious to see how this young minister and his wife lived. These farmers had probably never had a minister living so close to them before. Elsie and Lloyd got dressed in the quickest and most careful way possible, and then Elsie fixed their breakfast. They ate very simply because Lloyd's salary was quite small.

Of course, Elsie had to bring their water from the well to wash the dishes and clean her home. She also had to wash their clothes by hand using a wash tub and scrubbing board. When she was done, she took them outside and hung them out to dry just as her Mama had done years ago. She was so incredibly happy, and she was doing the work for her own family and in her own way. No more beatings, no more harsh words, she had no more fear.

Elsie was very frugal and did not buy anything that was not absolutely necessary but sometimes their meals were quite skimpy. Sometimes one of the farmers would bring them a few potatoes, or some other garden produce. Sometimes the farmers brought them some eggs or a quart of milk or a small jar of cream. All these were sacrificial gifts from these poor folks and Elsie and Lloyd greatly appreciated the food given to them.

Lloyd and Elsie worked hard. They loved the people. And Lloyd was so happy to finally be a minister just like his dad. He visited the people in their homes and encouraged them whenever he could. Lloyd was a good minister and God helped him prepare interesting sermons. Elsie loved children so she would tell the children Bible stories. In that way the children felt welcome at church and that the church was not only for the adults, but the children belonged there and it for them also.

Lloyd also loved working with the young people, and he tried to do special things just for them. Lloyd even got the idea to have a special camp just for the young people. It was not big or fancy, but he was able to find a few tents where the young people could sleep. These camps were only for a few days because most of the young folks needed to help on their family farms. It was the first time any "junior camps" were held anywhere in that area, but it was a beginning.

"Junior camp" usually means boys and girls ages 10-15. But at this first camp there were not really any young juniors as most of the people who came were young people in their late teens to early twenties. Parents did not want their young children to go off alone gallivanting under who knew what circumstances.

Lloyd had to persuade some of the farmers to let their young people go to such a new-fangled thing as "junior camp." Not all the young folks were allowed to go but enough went so that there was a good camp. The young folks met other young people their age. Games were played, it was almost like recess at school. No one had to do their heavy farm chores for a few days, there were Bible classes and new things learned about the Bible, the campers enjoyed playing games outside; and in the evenings, there was a campfire and interesting stories. When those who had been at camp came home, they were so happy and had had such a good time that it made others want to go also. Lloyd had started a new custom! There would be one camp every year.

The little churches in that district prospered. People noticed what diligent workers Elsie and Lloyd were and it wasn't long before the elders at the conference office who were in charge of the churches in that area asked Lloyd to go to a different area. They gave him more churches and a larger district. No matter where he went, he always tried to do something special for the young people and Elsie helped to make church interesting for the children. They were young, Lloyd enjoyed his work and Elsie was a good help to him. They were a good team.

One day, sometime late in 1939, after Lloyd and Elsie had become established in their new district, Lloyd received notice that the conference was going to be sending a visiting minister to his district. This minister's name was Elder Haener, he was an older gentleman and a very experienced minister. It would be a real privilege to have him come and visit Lloyd's churches. The conference told Lloyd that since he had a car, they wanted him to take care of Elder Haener and Lloyd was to be sure that Elder Haener got to visit all the churches in the district.

The day came and Lloyd went to the train station to meet Elder Haener and the two of them got into Lloyd's car and away they went. The churches were so blessed to have this gentleman visit them and the people certainly enjoyed the talks he gave. It was a privilege for Lloyd to listen to the visiting minister talk at the different churches. When they were done in one place, the two of them would get into the car drive to another church in a different area. Lloyd and Elder Haener spent several days doing this and as they drove along, they would talk. Lloyd enjoyed hearing of the experiences Elder Haener shared with him and he also felt that he was learning a lot from this older, well-experienced minister.

One day as the two of them were driving along and chatting, suddenly Elder Haener asked, "Lloyd, did your dad ever tell you how he learned that the seventh day is the Sabbath of the Bible, and that God wants us to keep it holy?" Lloyd had never heard the story, so he was happy to listen to the facts that Elder Haener told him. This is the story he told Lloyd.

"Many years ago, there was a family who lived in Germany. Andrew was the father of this family. He along with his wife and six children had been reading the Bible but could not understand what all it meant Andrew had discovered that there was a group in Poland who followed all of the teachings of the Bible, so Andrew decided to write a letter to the office headquarters of this group and ask if there was someone who could please be sent to Germany and help his family to study and understand what the Bible was saying to them. In 1897 I was a young minister in Poland, when Andrew's letter arrived at the office asking for help. He asked if a minister could please be sent to teach them and help them understand."

Poland and Germany shared a border, but due to the various wars the border had shifted several times. Elder Haener did not tell Lloyd what part of Poland he lived in or what part of Germany Andrew's family lived in. From the details Elder Haener shared with Lloyd, it was obvious that there was quite a distance between these two areas.

Elder Haener continued that "at that time there were not many ministers in Poland and all of them had several positions to fill. When this letter arrived, for one reason or another each minister had a valid reason why he could not make the journey. It seemed no one was available to answer this call for help. Even though I was a young minister, I felt a real need to answer this call. I did not have much money, in fact I was so poor, I did not own a buggy, I did not even own my own horse, and I certainly could not afford to buy a train ticket. But I was young, and I did have two good legs, so I decided I would walk to the part of Germany where this family lived. I wore the best clothes I had, I took my Bible and wrapped it carefully to protect it and I set out on my walk.

"I walked and I walked, and I walked some more. I wore holes in the soles of my shoes. I had no money to buy another pair, so I just found some heavy cardboard and stuffed it inside of my shoes and I kept walking. Every time the cardboard wore out, I would replace it with more cardboard, and I kept walking. I washed as best I could in the little creeks I crossed and when evening came, I just slept on the ground in the woods, or if I were lucky, in some farmer's barn. Food was not plentiful, but I ate what I could find and sometimes a farmer would offer me a meal.

"It took me three weeks of walking many miles every day, but I finally arrived at the out-skirts of the small village where Andrew and his family lived. I put some new cardboard in my shoes and stopped in the woods to pat down my hair and brush off my clothes a bit so that I would be presentable to them.

"I had brushed the travel dust and straw off of my clothes the best I could, but when I looked at myself, I thought I looked like a mess! I came here to teach the Bible; I am representing God to these people. I do not look good enough; I am not a good representative of God. I am dirty, my clothes are dirty, I look too bad. No, I cannot go meet somebody and talk about God looking like this. So, I turned around, went back to the road, and started my walk back to Poland.

"As I walked, I began to think. These people want to study the Bible; these people want to know about God. I have walked three weeks to come and teach them and now that I have finally arrived, I have turned my back on them and am going home. Is that what God would want me to do? So, I decided I would do what I had come to do, and I turned around again and walked into the village.

"After asking about Andrew's family, I was told where their house was. It was a typical country village house of that time. It was long and about one room deep. The animals were housed at one end of the house and the family lived in the other end on the other side of a dividing wall. This was a good arrangement as it made it easy to care for the animals in the winter since the farmer did not need to go outside in the bitter cold to get to the barn. Also, the warmth of the animals helped to keep the part of the house where the family lived warmer in the cold winters. In the summer, when it was warmer, the animals were kept outside where there was a shelter for them.

"When I knocked on the door of the home, a young boy of five years old answered my knock. I greeted him and asked if his father was at home. The little boy said, 'No, he's out working in the field, but my mama is here.' The small boy called his mama and I introduced myself to her and stated my reason for being at their door that morning. Immediately she sent the little boy out to the field to call Andrew, his papa. Lloyd, that five-year-old boy who answered my knock was named Samuel, he's your dad now.

"As soon as the father, Andrew, got to the house, I introduced myself to him and he and his wife sat right down at the kitchen table, and we started to study the Bible. We studied all the rest of that day. That evening we stopped only for a quick meal and to care for the animals and then we went right back to studying. We studied until it got dark, and we had to light the lamps, then we kept right on studying and we studied all that night.

"Before the sun came up the next morning Andrew and his wife decided that since they had learned God is not a vengeful God, but a totally loving God and He really loved them so much He sent Jesus to die for their sins, they wanted to show their love to Him by honoring Him so had chosen to obey Him completely and do exactly what the Bible says. Therefore, they had decided to keep the seventh day holy even though they did not know anyone else who worshipped on the seventh day. They also asked if they could be baptized.

"This family was so anxious to learn what the Bible really teaches that as soon as the chores were done, and we had eaten a quick meal we sat down and began studying again. The only church in the village was the state church but they decided that it did not matter if they were the only ones in the village following the Bible. They wanted to follow exactly what the Bible taught. So, after a few days of studying with them, I baptized them and then I walked back to Poland."

As often happened in those times, as a boy got into his teens, he would hire himself out to help a farmer in a different locality. This is what Fred had done. Fred was Samuel's oldest brother. Fred had been gone working when Elder Haener had visited Samuel's parents. When he came home and saw the change in his family and observed the different way they were living, he became very angry. He said, "You have become Jews! I want nothing to do with this Jew religion. I will not live in this house anymore." He had friends in the village, and he asked to live with one of them. This family welcomed him into their home.

After a few days, his friend's parents asked him why he wasn't living at home with his family anymore. When Fred explained the changes his parents had made and how they were living, the father and mother spoke very seriously to Fred. Back then, young folks listened to their elders and when parents or other elders talked to you, you listened, and you did what they said. And so, Fred listened to these friends. They said, "Fred, you may not agree with your parents, but they are your parents, and you must respect them. It is your duty to go back home and live with them and help them, even if you do not agree with their choices." Therefore, Fred moved back home with his family.

Fred didn't say much but he observed his family closely. They seemed so very happy. Everything was different. Their way of worship had changed, the day on which they worshipped God had changed, their diet had changed. It didn't matter that they were the only ones in their village living like this.

He also learned that they were definitely not Jews. He discovered that they loved Jesus more than they ever had. As Fred watched and listened, he discovered that Jesus was the very center of everything they did. Soon, he too, began to read the Bible and as he read and learned what the Bible really says, he also began to live like they did. And the family was united again.

A few years later Fred got itchy feet and decided he wanted to leave this small town. He had heard so much about America, so he set his sights on going to that great land. He worked hard and saved his money very carefully. It took him awhile, but eventually he had saved enough money to buy a one-way ticket on a boat going to America. He settled in North Dakota as there were several other German people living in that area.

Soon letters began arriving back in Germany about this wonderful land of opportunity. Fred told his family that all of them should come to this wonderful country also. The land was very fertile, was cheap, and freely available to all who would improve it. It was good farming country. Another advantage of this country of America was that it had religious freedom, and everyone could choose to worship how he/she wanted, and no one would bother you or make fun of you.

Father Andrew and Mother talked about it and decided that Fred was right and began saving their money so that their whole family could buy boat tickets to come to the great country of America. After saving for a few years, they had saved enough money so that when their farm, farm equipment, animals, furniture, and all their things were sold, there was enough money to pay for their one-way boat tickets so the rest of their family could all come to America together. Now they would be united as a family again with all their four boys and two girls.

Samuel was fifteen years old when he arrived in this country. He began to have desires of his own. He had seen the happy changes that had been made in his family and he decided that he wanted to be a minister so that he could teach others how much God loved them and how to be really happy in obeying Jesus exactly as the Bible teaches. But Father Andrew had other ideas. He said, "Fred is the oldest son, he will be the minister. Samuel, you will be a farmer like me." Samuel was very disappointed. But he had to do what his father said.

A few years later, Samuel met a young lady, Lydia who had also come from Germany with her parents. Lydia's family arrived in America in 1899 when she was just two years old. Lydia was kind, gentle, generous, loved Jesus with all of her heart, and was a very hard worker. It soon became obvious that Samuel was more than a little interested in Lydia. In 1914 Samuel and Lydia were married. She was just seventeen years old when they got married, Samuel was twenty-two. They were able to rent and settle on a small farm close to his parents and began farming.

Samuel simply was not happy, he had one great desire. He wanted to be a minister. Oh, how he wanted to tell others about Jesus' great love. Even though Samuel was now married, had his own wife, and his own place, even though it was rented, he still had to listen to his father and his father always said, "No, you will be a farmer like me. Fred is the oldest he will be the preacher."

Now there was a problem. It so happened that Fred did not want to be a preacher! He wanted to travel to other places and see other things. He learned that he could sell Christian books and travel to other places. This satisfied his father, so Fred became a book salesman. He would go to an area and sell books and teach the people who were interested. When there was a small, interested group of people he would call for a minister to come and establish a church there and Fred would move on to another area. So even though he was not a regular minister, he was helping people to learn about Jesus and what the Bible teaches. Father Andrew was happy with Fred's choice.

Samuel believed without a doubt that God had called him to be a minister and he just wanted to preach. He talked it over with Lydia. She always said she would help him no matter what he did. Samuel struggled on trying to farm, but he was not happy. A year after he and Lydia were married, on June 12, 1915, they had a baby son and they named him Lloyd. For a few years Samuel struggled on with the farm, but his heart was not in it, he felt that God's desire for him was that he should be a minister. He knew in his heart that God had called him, and he could not say "no" to God. What should he do? Honor his father, Andrew, or try to honor his Father in heaven by becoming a pastor as he felt called to do?

Samuel struggled on trying to be a farmer for approximately 3 more years. Finally, he could take it no longer. After much prayer, and many long intense discussions, Samuel and Lydia decided that they would farm for one more year, if it was a good year, they would sell everything, take the money and go to school where he could study how to become a minister. They decided not to tell anyone about their decision. This was only between them and God. It would not be easy, but they believed they could make it work.

So, for another year he put in his crops and waited for the harvest, and what a year it was! That harvest was the best he had ever had. Everyone was amazed at their great harvest. They all said, "Now, you see, you are to be a real farmer!" But to everyone's surprise he said, "No, we are going to go to school, and I am going to become a minister." It was hard for Andrew to see Samuel make his own choice.

After the crops were harvested and they had sold what little farm equipment was theirs, he and Lydia packed up their meager belongings and their young son Lloyd, who was almost five years old at this time and their young family of three moved to Missouri. At that time there was a German seminary there and that is where Samuel went to school. It was not easy for them, Lydia worked as the cook for the school so that she could help Samuel with his tuition. After one year, several of the teachers told him, "Samuel, you know more about the Bible than we do. You must go out and preach." And that is what he did until the day he died.

Because Samuel loved God so much that he gave up everything to become a minister, there are people in churches which he helped to start all across North Dakota, South Dakota, Nebraska, and parts of Canada. Today the fourth generation of Samuel's family are still sharing the love of Jesus with others.

Because a young man wanted to do something for God and was willing to walk three weeks just to study the Bible with one family there are hundreds of people who came to know, love, and worship God. Samuel wasn't the only one of Andrew's sons who became a minister. Another of Andrew's sons, Ben, also became a minister, Fred sold Christian books, and the fourth son, Jake, became a farmer.

When Elder Haener gets to heaven, he will certainly be amazed to see the results of his long walk just to help one family study the Bible. It has been just like ripples when a stone is dropped into in a quiet pond. Today the ripples are still growing because many of the families who came to believe in the God of the Bible had sons who grew up and became ministers in many parts of the world.

Hearing this story helped Lloyd to better understand his dad's strong desire to help as many people as he could even when it meant great sacrifices for him and his family and even though his life was threatened many times. Elsie could also understand Lloyd's strong desire to follow in his dad's footsteps.

Shortly after the time when Elder Haener came to visit Lloyd's district, Elsie and Lloyd had an addition to their family. In early 1940 a baby daughter was born to them. Elsie had read a story about a girl named Carol whose name meant song of God and she decided that is what she wanted to name her daughter. They gave her a middle name of Joy because they wanted her to always be a joyful song of God.

About two and a half years after Carol was born, they had another daughter and named her Lou. So now their family was complete. Elsie stayed home to take care of their girls and Lloyd concentrated on his work as a minister. Elsie loved children and she always helped with the children at church. It seemed like things were going well, and they were settling into being a young family. They were so very happy.

Then one day a large envelope came to their house. It was from the General Conference, the world headquarters of their church. What could they want? When Lloyd opened the envelope, he was quite surprised. He read that they were asking him to go as a missionary to South America.

South America! That's a strange place to send two people of German background who spoke German fluently and who both talked English just as fluently and neither of them knowing a word of Spanish. Neither of them even know how to say "yes" or "no" in Spanish! And they had two little girls: one almost three and the other just a couple of months old. What should they do? Lloyd respected his dad and wanted to be near to him. Elsie loved his mother and dad, and they had two granddaughters whom the grandparents loved with all their hearts.

To complicate matters, it was in the middle of a terrible war. Could they even travel safely at that time? Lloyd and Elsie believed that if God called them to go somewhere they should answer that call. They prayed about the letter and talked it over and they decided that if God opened the door for them to go, they would walk through it in faith, and He would take care of the details.

Chapter Six

Lloyd and Elsie told Mother and Dad of their call to the mission field and that they had decided to answer, "yes." Then came many days of making serious plans for a long and complicated move. The family had no idea what a big change this would make in their lives, neither did Mother and Dad. However, everything familiar was willingly left behind to happily begin a new life in an as yet unknown, to them, country. There were passports, visas, shots, and all types of other documents which were needed not only for Lloyd and Elsie but also for their two girls.

There were so very many questions; do we need to bring a refrigerator, or a stove, or any large appliances like that? The definite answer was, "No, you can get all of that there." Therefore, all of those large appliances were left behind. No one bothered to tell them that the appliances that were available over there were three or four times as expensive and the quality was very poor. Elsie and Lloyd knew they were leaving for seven years or longer so whatever came with them had to do for many years. Another big question was whether they would ever come back. Communication and distances were so very different in the early 1940's than they are now.

It took a long time for them to get everything ready. It was war time, and everything was concentrated on the war effort and soldiers and the things they needed always took precedence. Ordinary people had to wait, it seemed their needs and desires came low on the list. Lloyd got large wooden crates and packed all of his books, their kettles, some dishes, some linens, necessities for the baby (there were no disposable diapers back then), and a small doll for Carol. This was all so new and strange to them and not one of them had any idea what would be available to them where they were going. When the crates were full, Lloyd nailed them shut. Then the wooden crates were sent to a storage place in New York to await the orders and space to send them overseas.

At the last-minute Elsie decided she had better take a duffle bag, that was a large heavy-duty canvass bag, and she decided to put into it a couple of sheets and towels, "just in case." Just in case of what she did not know. She also put in some clothes and a few other things. This could be thrown around just about anywhere but would go with their suitcases and arrive with them.

Finally, they had their passports, permissions to travel and all their things ready to go. The four of them said goodbye to Elsie's family in Canada. Last of all they went to visit Mother and Dad who lived in Pittsburgh at that time. The plans were to spend a few days there before travelling south to Miami to get on the airplane. A few days turned into weeks, then months. There was a war, and missionaries did not take priority. The four of them waited and waited and waited some more. Of course, Mother and Dad loved having a prolonged visit with their granddaughters and spending a few extra weeks with Lloyd and Elsie. No one knew when or even if they would ever see each other again.

This was a commitment for life. They were going a long way away, there was a war going on, and Germans were considered enemies. No one mentioned the fact that they were of German descent. Lloyd and Elsie both had American passports. Lloyd had been born in North Dakota, and Elsie's father and mother had been born in America, so she was able to qualify as "American" also. But in the back of their minds was always the fact that their heritage was German.

Mother and Dad were not getting any younger. It was a bittersweet time for them all. Mother and Dad were so proud of Lloyd and Elsie, but it was still a big sacrifice to give up their children and grandchildren. None of them knew whether they would ever see each other again. And it was so hard for Mother and Dad to let those precious little girls go off to who-knows-where. The girls were growing so fast; Mother and Dad would miss so many of their normal adventures of growing up. Telephones were not so common then as now. Mail took months to go or come. Internet and computers were unheard of. Family and friends would truly be isolated from each other.

Finally, the day came when they had all their permissions to travel and visas to live in the foreign country. None of them knew what the future held but they were happy to be on their way as "real" missionaries. Dad drove them to the train station and Mother and Dad stood on the platform as Lloyd, Elsie, and the little girls boarded the train they were to ride all the way from Pittsburg to Miami. The train was crowded with soldiers, every seat was occupied, and many were even standing in the aisles. One of the soldiers took pity on Elsie standing and holding the baby with one arm while trying to keep track of Carol with her other hand so he got up and offered her his seat. When Elsie gratefully sat down, Carol squeezed in beside her while Elsie held the baby. Lloyd had to stand. Suitcases and duffle bags were everywhere, and some soldiers used their duffle bags as seats. It was an interesting train ride.

Eventually the four of them got to Miami, there they spent the night in a hotel and then were taken to the plane the next day. It was quite a plane! It was a sea plane, and it had to land and take off from the ocean. It was not very big, but the back end opened upwards and then they walked down into the belly of the plane. Because it was war time and they would be flying outside of American territory, all the windows were blackened out with black paper. You could not see out at all. When the door was shut it was dark. Seats were cramped and close together, there was no air conditioning. The passengers just sat there, waiting to take off. This was the first plane ride for the four of them, and they were not sure what to expect, what was normal, or what was not.

With the door closed and everything all dark it soon got quite hot. The little family were used to Canadian weather and none of them had ever experienced heat like this or such high humidity. The little plane sitting on the water was just like a little boat bouncing up and down and up and down, over and over. Soon some of the people began to get seasick. The airplane had provided bags which people could use, but oh, the smell was almost unbearable. No one told them why the takeoff was delayed, or what other problem or problems were causing the delay but finally plane was able to take off.

It was very hard on the baby; she was too small to understand why her little world had changed so much. She was most uncomfortable and cried and cried. Of course, some of the passengers did not appreciate the crying baby. And no one appreciated the smell made by those who were seasick, but no one could help that either. Lloyd and Elsie were learning the joys of being missionaries and the adaptability required of them.

It was better once the plane was in the air. After several hours they arrived in Jamaica. Here the passengers were allowed to get off of the plane and go into the airport for a little while. It was so good to be able to stand up, stretch, and move around on firm ground again. Lloyd, Elsie and Carol were even offered some lemonade to drink. But oh, what humidity and heat. None of them had ever even dreamed that they could be so hot, sweaty, and sticky all at the same time. This certainly was very different than Canada!

It seemed like too soon they were in the tiny, hot, dark belly of the plane again. It was like being in a small boat, all closed in, and it just went up and down on the water. Eventually the plane took off again and they were on the last leg of their trip in the sea plane. The take-off and landing were rather frightening. They could not see anything. They could hear the water rushing over the wings and hear the motors. However, being unable to see what was happening did not help matters at all. In just 12 hours, Elsie's poor little baby had gone from being comfortable to being covered in a red prickly heat rash. She couldn't scratch, they had nothing to put on it to soothe it and she cried and cried.

Eventually they landed at the seacoast of Colombia, for that is where they were to serve. But they still had one more plane ride until arriving at their destination. The next plane was also rather small, but it was able to take off and land on the runway and they could see out of the windows. It climbed into the air and went up above the Andes mountains and soon they landed in the beautiful city of Medellin which was to be their home. It was high enough in the mountains that the weather was just perfect. The city of Medellin was surrounded by mountains and the scenery was spectacular.

Sadly, they learned that three weeks after they got off that little seaplane it went down while trying to land and all on board were killed. Flying in that type of sea plane back then was extremely dangerous, so they praised God for protecting them on their journey just three weeks previously.

Lloyd was to oversee the educational and young people's departments so he would have his own office. When he was home, he would go to the office every day. He was also expected to travel a lot and visit outlying areas and preach. Because missionaries were not really desired in the country, he could not put on his papers that he was a missionary. Missionaries were considered undesirable heretics. The state church controlled everything, and they believed and taught that anyone who believed and/or taught differently than they did was a heretic. Therefore, Lloyd had to put "teacher" on his papers. That was the true reason for his being there, he was to teach people about the true love of Jesus, and he was overseer of the educational department.

When Elsie, Lloyd and girls landed in Medellin, someone from the office met them and took them to the office. This gentleman told them that is where their family would live until they could find a house and their things which were in the crates which had been shipped by boat, arrived in the country.

At one time this office had been a large house and was built in the style of Latin homes. There was a lovely patio in the center, which was open to the sky. All around that patio were individual rooms in which the people lived. It was like having the outdoors come inside, but you were private and protected from things going on outside. This had been a lovely big house and had two patios. When it had been a private residence the family had lived in the front part and had the front patio. Now those rooms were used for the different offices. The back patio was not so large it was where the servants had lived and where the washing and cooking had been done and some of the rooms were used for storage. This back part is where Elsie, Lloyd, and their girls were to live until they found a house and their belongings arrived.

Elsie and Lloyd were very surprised to discover that every other family connected to the office was quite old compared to themselves. In fact, Elsie and Lloyd were the youngest ones there. The family closest to their ages had a daughter in college! One other young family who had small children had been there but after just a few weeks they had decided to return to America.

Elsie and Lloyd were taken to the back patio and shown an empty room. They were told this was where their family could live. Several of the rooms around this patio were still used for storage. There was a cement sink open to the patio where Elsie could wash their dishes and clothes, she could also cook in that area.

The person who brought them to the office told them that one of the rooms had several mattresses in it and they were welcome to put them on the floor of the room in which they were to live and then could sleep on them at night. It was already evening so Lloyd turned on the electric light and took a mattress and pulled it from the pile and started to take it into their room. As soon as he removed it from the pile, it came to life! It was absolutely full of bedbugs, and they scurried everywhere to hide from the light. Every mattress he tried was the same. He talked to someone about it and was told. Oh, that's okay, wait until morning and then lay the mattresses out in the patio in the sunshine and you will get rid of the bugs! It proved to be an interesting night and the first thing in the morning Lloyd put the mattresses out in the sunshine in the patio and the bugs did leave!

One of their first goals upon getting settled into their temporary quarters was to try to learn some Spanish. They even had to learn to say "yes" and "no." Since they both spoke German fluently and some of the rules of grammar for Spanish were similar to the German rules, they felt they had a little help getting started. It was still a great challenge for them. After three to four weeks the brethren decided that it was time for Lloyd to make a partial tour of their territory. He was to be gone for three weeks. This was rather hard on him. And it was also hard on Elsie, who was responsible for two little girls while still struggling with the language. But everyone survived and adjusted, and they did learn the language. The whole family learned to speak that beautiful language fluently, in fact the baby learned Spanish before she learned English.

Chapter Seven

When Lloyd returned from his trip, he began to search for their own home. This was another interesting experience. One Friday afternoon Elsie and Lloyd finally found a house that seemed like it would suit their needs and was affordable on their small budget. The owner of the house was very glad to rent to "Americans." But since it was getting late, the owner suggested that they meet in the lawyer's office to sign the papers the next morning, Sabado (Sabbath in English, named Saturday on the English calendar). Lloyd told him he was sorry, but he would not be able to make it at that time. Therefore, they agreed to meet first thing on Monday morning. Elsie and Lloyd were both so glad to know that their family would finally be able to move out of their one room and into a real house, even though it did not have any furniture and their belongings had not yet arrived. It would be their own private space.

They had a happy Sabbath and first thing on Monday morning Lloyd went to the lawyer's office. He was surprised to find the homeowner was not there and the lawyer told him, "You cannot have that house." The lawyer would not give Lloyd any details; he just said, "you will not be able to rent that house." That was quite a disappointment to say the least.

Just as Lloyd got outside onto the sidewalk, the American ambassador was walking by, and he stopped to chat and see how things were going. Lloyd told him about their disappointing experience with the house. The ambassador suggested he would investigate and see if he could discover what had happened to cause the change in plans. After the American ambassador had done some investigating, he was able to give Lloyd the details.

Friday evening the house owner had gone home and happily told his wife that he had rented their house and they both celebrated, especially since it was to an American! The houseowner and his wife presumed that Lloyd was a rich American oil man, and they knew Lloyd and his family would be good renters! The wife was a devout church goer and early the next morning (Sabado) when she went to daily Mass as was her custom, she quickly and happily told the priest of their great blessing in renting the house to an American.

The priest was not so thrilled. He began to ask questions. "Was the man smoking?" "No." "Was the wife wearing lots of jewelry? "No." Did she smoke?" "Well, no." Was she dressed very nicely and painted up with lots of make-up?" "Well, no." "Did he curse and swear?" "No." After a few such questions and answers the priest said, "They are heretics, and you cannot rent to them. You will have to have a special ceremony to remove all the evil spirits they left in your house because they walked through it."

The people were used to obeying whatever the priests told them to do, so that meant Lloyd and Elsie did not get their house. After some more searching Elsie and Lloyd did find a house in that same neighborhood and not too far from the original house so they learned what had happened at the original house which should have been their home. The priest had a special ceremony at the house, he came in and walked through the house and sprinkled holy water in each room, each corner, and every part of the house to get rid of the evil spirits that had contaminated their house because heretics had walked through it.

Then to be sure that the house was really protected from the evil influences, the priest had the lady and her husband erect a special statue of the virgin Mary in the front yard. The ceremony to cast the evil spirits out of the house was not cheap. Those poor house-owners had to pay a large fee to the priest who performed the ceremony. Twenty-five years later when Lloyd was visiting the area, he was able to drive by the house and the statue was still there, so it seems that the house had been cleaned and protected from the evil spirits left by the heretics.

The family enjoyed the house that they were able to rent. It had very high walls all around the back "yard" which was mostly cement, but there was also a small patch of grass. There were good clothes lines where Elsie could hang their laundry to dry. That was one reason for the high walls around it. Several times a long pole with a hook on the end of it could be seen coming over the wall. Someone on the outside was reaching over the wall trying to pick clothes off of the line. That trick never worked; the wall was too high.

The front yard was small but also had a nice patch of green grass. This was surrounded by a low cement wall. The yard was a bit protected, but you could climb over the low wall and the girls enjoyed running around there when their Daddy was outside with them. The girls were not allowed out there alone. There was a walkway along one side, with geraniums growing all along the side of the walkway. There were a few steps leading up to where the front door was located. The front door was back from the street at the side of the house, and faced the raised area where the geraniums were growing.

One day Lloyd was outside trimming the geraniums at the side of the house, and he allowed the girls to come out and be in the front yard while he was there and could keep an eye on them. It was mid to late afternoon and the children from the local parochial school were on their way home from school. All of a sudden Carol started to cry. Lloyd looked up from his work just in time to see one of the local schoolgirls hitting Carol. Acting quicker than it takes to tell, Lloyd was by her side and took hold of the girl's arm to stop her from hitting Carol. Immediately the girl started to cry and said, "No me chupas la sangre, no me chupas la sangre." Lloyd told her he had no intention of sucking her blood, he just wanted her to stop hitting and hurting his daughter! Wanting to keep their parishioners away from the "heretics" living amongst them, the priests had told the locals all kinds of evil things which would happen to them if they let the "heretics" come too close to them.

The next afternoon Lloyd was outside finishing his trimming of the plants in the front and again the two girls were out there with him. This day the schoolgirls stopped to talk with them. The girls asked, "would you like to know what happened to the girl you stopped from hitting your daughter yesterday?" Of course, he was interested. Then the girls said when we got to school this morning the nuns questioned us as to what happened on our way home from school yesterday. When the nuns learned the story, the poor girl was scolded, punished, and made to do penance by kneeling in front of the whole class all day long! The girl was not punished because she had hurt someone but because she had been discovered doing it. The locals were taught to hurt and harass the "heretics" in any way possible but were never to get discovered or caught at it. Whatever damage the local people could do to a heretic would guarantee their dead loved ones could get out of purgatory quicker, the more damage done, the sooner the release would come.

Life was certainly different than anything Elsie and Lloyd had ever known, and it was very interesting. It took most of a year, 51 weeks to be exact, for their boxes and crates to arrive. Their shipment had actually arrived some time before that, but it had to go through customs and be approved to be able to stay in the country legally.

Elsie and Lloyd were so glad to finally get their things, Lloyd had especially missed his books. When the boxes were opened, what a shock was theirs! Someone in customs had discovered that these crates and boxes belonged to heretics, so the customs person had opened the boxes and poured a very foul-smelling liquid over all their things. Elsie and Lloyd knew a customs agent had done the damage because where the boxes were stored in the United States no one would have done something like that. When the boxes were in transit the shipping company had so many containers, they were too busy to bother with opening a few boxes and destroying the contents. When persons were missionaries, you quickly learned that the state church taught its adherents that doing harm to a heretic would lessen your time in purgatory. This information was shared by people who had done harm to missionaries before they had learned about what Jesus was truly like.

That smelly liquid which had been poured over everything, had saturated his books, staining them and the books reeked of that awful smell. Lloyd set them out in the fresh air to try to clean them up and it helped a little bit, but 75 years later the books were still stained, and although it was not as strong as originally, things still smelled of that odor. The fabric things were also stained and smelly. Even though the clothes and anything fabric were washed, they were stained. Carol was so disappointed to see her cherished doll. It was a small rubber one, but she did not have many toys and it was special to her. The poor doll's arms, legs, and body had been totally melted by that liquid. It was just a gooey, sticky, stinky mess.

Some people did not want the heretics in their country, but there were many lovely people who were so glad that the missionaries had come. The local people were so glad that there is a loving God who takes care of His people.

It was such good news that they could worship a kind, loving God and not one who was waiting to take vengeance on them for each little mistake but would gladly forgive them. This loving God did not require money in order for Him to give His forgiveness; neither did this loving God require penances. It hurt to have to walk on your knees for a long way just to satisfy the harsh requirements of the God which the people were accustomed to worshipping.

It was a hard time to try to tell people about Jesus and even the local people who were glad to hear about this loving God often suffered persecution from their former friends and even their families who just did not understand the change in their beliefs about this loving God. How could God love and care for His people and not require money when they were poor, or require things hard for them to do in order to receive His acceptance?

Going to the market to buy food was another challenge where Elsie learned to change some of her customs. Until she could speak Spanish fluently, usually one of the local people who loved them would go along to help. The seller would see an American and the price immediately jumped up several times. The local person would say that is too much and offer much less than the seller had asked. It would go back and forth until a fair price was established. After Elsie learned the language, she could do her own bargaining. The sellers soon learned that she was not a rich tourist but someone who lived there all the time and it became easier for her to go shopping.

Market day was different in other ways also. There were so many new customs. You did not wear your best clothes, and you did not wear your best shoes! You took along a large "bolsa" (bag). It was usually strong cloth or woven plastic with strong handles. When you got to the market you had to find the items you needed. You went to one of several fruit sellers to buy oranges, pineapple, bananas, and many other delicious and unique tropical fruits. You had to go to a different seller to buy rice or beans, and oh what a variety of beans there were. They had red ones, black ones, white ones, spotted ones, brown ones, lentils, garbanzos, all kinds of things that Elsie had never seen on the farm. These items were usually found in large "gunny sacks" sitting on the floor and you would simply tell the seller how much you wanted. Then the seller would weigh that amount out, and put it on a piece of newspaper, twist it tightly shut, then you would add the little bundle of beans, salt, rice or whatever it was to the things already in your bolsa.

If you wanted fresh vegetables, you went to the seller who had fresh vegetables and repeated the process. These were usually stacked right on the floor, or on small tables. There were no canned foods and certainly no frozen ones! If you wanted eggs, you went to the person who had poultry and eggs and the eggs, too, were wrapped in small packages. There was no way to tell how fresh the eggs were. Going grocery shopping was a long process for Elsie that took all morning, and sometimes part of the afternoon also. It was always an interesting adventure.

You had to be careful where you stepped as people often spit right on the floor, chickens often ran loose, and you had to avoid the mess they left. For those who ate chicken at least they knew it was fresh because it was still alive when they bought it. Then they took it home and had to kill it, pluck the feathers off, and prepare it in order to get it ready to eat. Vegetable sellers would also throw rotten or damaged goods on the floor. All in all, navigating the market was always a challenging experience for Elsie.

After shopping, the first thing she did when she got home, was to take off her shoes and leave them on the back porch. On one of her early trips to the market, she purchased several different types of beans as she didn't know what the difference was between all the varieties. She left the heavy things like oranges and pineapples in the sink outside to be washed before being brought into the house. Then she placed the little bundles of beans on top of the kitchen counter while she went upstairs to change her dress. When she came back downstairs the white counter was alive with little black bugs. The beans were full of live, extra protein.

Elsie soon learned how to deal with the different foodstuffs. All the beans and rice had to be sorted by hand to remove all the small stones, the live bugs, and even the beans which had holes or even bug eggs in them. All the vegetables had to be thoroughly scrubbed, and anything fresh had to be disinfected before it could be eaten. Even when there was corn on the cob, it had to be husked, the worms cut out, and then the whole cob soaked in water so the tiny white worms would come crawling out of the individual kernels. It was all quite a challenge. The market as Lloyd and Elsie found it in the early 1940's was very different than it is in Medellin today.

All the water had to be boiled before the family could drink it or put it into their mouths. The pasteurized milk which was purchased had to be strained to remove bugs, hair, or other foreign material and it too, had to be boiled. Lloyd used to jokingly say, "Yes, it is pasteurized because the cow that gave it was in the pasture, and the bull who carried the milk cans to the market was also in the pasture."

Often more than half of the "fresh" eggs which Elsie brought home from the market would have small chicks at all different stages of development in them. Other times when she would crack open an egg, it smelled so rotten that it could only be thrown out. Lloyd and Elsie decided the only way to know that their eggs were fresh was to buy 6 young chickens and raise them and feed them good grain and then gather their own eggs. So, Lloyd built a small chicken coop in the back yard and soon the family was enjoying their own good fresh eggs.

Absolutely everything had to be made from scratch. All the produce and veggies cleaned and disinfected, then Elsie could start preparing the meals. The floors had to be disinfected, the clothes washed, hung outside to dry, and then ironed. There were no easy-care fabrics and all the little cotton dresses, Lloyd's shirts and Elsie's dresses had to be ironed by hand. There was a lot of work in taking care of the two little girls and protecting them from picking up too many germs. She also did all the things a missionary wife was expected to do. It was obvious that Elsie needed some help in her home.

When Lloyd was not out traveling but was able to be at home, he was often asked to preach at one of the many churches in Medellin. Since he had to be away from home so often, when he was at home and asked to preach at one of the local churches, Elsie and the girls would always go with him so the family could worship together. At one of the churches Lloyd and Elsie attended, they became acquainted with a family who was very poor, this family had several children. One of the older girls was named Angela and she desperately wanted to go to school but there was just no way the family could afford to pay the tuition costs. The father was ill and could not work at all.

When Angela was a little girl, her family had lived on a huge banana plantation which was about 24 miles from the city of Bucaramanga, a city in Colombia. Her daddy was one of the plantation workers. It was such a big plantation and was so far from town that the plantation owners "helped" the workers by having some houses where the workers could live with their families right on the plantation. Plantation workers did not make much money and did not have cars so having houses on the plantation helped them and the owner could get more work out of them. There also a small store where the workers could buy staple foods, like rice, beans, sugar, flour, salt and a few other items like small candies, soda pop, and some beer. As the custom was, the items the workers purchased would be placed on newspaper, or small pieces of paper and be wrapped into little bundles. The plantation also provided a school for the workers' children. Angela was a happy person and loved to learn about people, places, and things that were different than on the plantation.

One day Angela's daddy started talking about some strange things he had heard. Did you know we are not to pray to idols because they cannot hear or see us? And certainly, they cannot answer us. Did you know that we can pray directly to God? Did you know that we do not have to do penances to have our sins forgiven? We do not have to buy candles to place in front of the images in church, or any of the shrines. He learned about God's special ten rules to help us live happier lives. Did you know that the seventh day is God's Sabado? He was learning so many other things the Bible taught. The more he learned, the more he became convinced that he wanted to live that way. He tried the best he knew how.

But Angela and her mother were not happy with him. Her mother tried to tell him he was wrong. He would show them from the Bible, but Mama always said, "the leader of the state church tells us to follow the traditions in the same way that our ancestors have done, and we have always done the same thing our ancestors did. That certainly cannot be wrong." Angela's mother and daddy had many long discussions and finally they came to an agreement. Daddy would pray his way and he would ask God to help Mama and Angela understand what the Bible taught about God and His love. Mama and Angela would pray the rosary the way they had been taught. They would pray that Daddy would come back to worship in the way which the state church taught and to follow the traditions which the church told the people to follow.

Angela and Mama would pray the Ave Marias, the Padre Nuestros, and the Misterios at each bead of the rosary. Daddy would just kneel down and pray like he was talking to a very good friend. It wasn't long before Angela and Mama began to think they were just making useless noises, but that Daddy prayed like he was talking to Someone who was real. Like he knew the Person he was talking to. After a short while Angela and her Mama began to worship with Daddy.

Many of the people were so very poor they did not have shoes to wear. When they began to go to church, they wanted to respect God, so they scrimped and saved, and each person was able to get one pair of shoes. The people did not wear these shoes during the week. They went barefooted everywhere. On Sabbath when they went to church, they would wrap their shoes in a newspaper and carry the shoes in their hands. When they got about two blocks from the church they would stop, take out their shoes and put them on so they could wear shoes in God's house. Ater church the people would walk about two blocks away from the church, stop and take off their shoes and wrap them up and carry them home so they could have shoes to wear for church next week.

Four years went by, and Angela was now fifteen years old and the little school on the plantation did not teach any higher level than what Angela had finished. Her parents decided that since she wanted to go to school so badly, they would take her into town, and she could board with a family friend. She would be able to attend a special girls' school run by Teacher Gomez.

Angela had only been keeping the seventh day Sabado for four years at this time, but she loved Jesus very much and she wanted to obey God's 10 special rules. During these years school went six days a week, from Monday through Sabado, so before she started school, she asked Teacher Gomez if she could be absent on Sabado. In Spanish there is only one word for the seventh day of the week and that is Sabado. They do not have two names (Sabbath or Saturday) like we do in English, for the seventh day of the week. The teacher was very kind and said, "Of course you may be absent on Sabado."

For some reason the teacher did not think to ask Angela, "Why?" Soon the teacher became used to having Angela being gone on Sabado and Angela was such a good student everything went along well for quite a while.

Several months later an American missionary who happened to be a friend of Lloyd's, came to town and held some meetings. He was a good speaker and spoke Spanish very fluently and many people came to hear him. There is something interesting that happens when people learn what the Bible really teaches. Many of them choose to obey the Bible and not just do what some person tells them to do, or just to keep following their traditions. That is exactly what happened in Bucaramanga during these meetings.

As often happens when people learn what the Bible teaches about God, that God is love, He is not vengeful, He is not waiting to punish anyone. You can pray right to God since He is your friend, you don't need to pray through a priest, you do not need to buy "globos" to send up in the night sky so that your prayers will get closer to God. It was so good not to have to do penances to receive forgiveness or spend money to buy relatives out of purgatory or spend money to buy candles to burn at the many shrines, or in front of the images in the churches. It was wonderful to learn to trust God and not to fear Him.

Of course, this made the leaders of the state church very unhappy. They began to criticize the missionary and to say things against the visiting missionary's church. The church leaders tried by many different ways to drive the evangelist out of their town, but something always happened to thwart their plans. The priest also asked his church members to pray that the curse of God would be on the meetings. However, that did not seem to work very well either.

One afternoon the visiting missionary was in the home with some of his friends with whom he was staying. While he was visiting with his friends, they heard a loud commotion outside. Looking out the windows they could see a large drunken mob coming down the street towards the house they were in. This mob was led by the priest and had a large pole with them. The men were carrying their machetes and the mob was screaming "down with the heretics."

When the mob arrived at the house, some of the larger men used the pole and banged into the door. The men battered on the door many times. The home was a humble one and the door was a simple door. The mob battered and battered on the door, but it just would not give in. The poor folks inside were trapped, there was no way of escape, they just prayed for God's protection. After an extended period of time, the priest and the mob dissipated and walked away. The visiting missionary went to open the door and look out to be sure all was quiet. When he touched the door, it fell off right into his hands.

Something else happened. Just to be sure everyone understood what was expected of them, one of the leaders of the state church decided to come to the school every morning and help the students with their morning prayers. The students were to say 10 Ave Marias, 10 Padre Nuestros, and 5 Misterios for each bead on their rosaries. Angela was in class when she heard someone tell the teacher this was going to happen. So immediately, she prayed quietly that God would help her be true to what the Bible says.

She had just finished her silent prayer, when the man from the state church came in and told everyone to kneel and start praying the way he taught them. Angela was very kind and thoughtful, she did not want to be disrespectful, so when everyone else knelt down to pray their rosaries, she quietly stood by her desk and bowed her head and silently prayed to God.

Just before the man left the classroom, he bent down and whispered something to the teacher.

The next day the same man came and led the students in saying prayers on the rosary but after the prayers the man taught a class in "religion," he made certain to carefully teach the students how wrong the missionary was by teaching people differently than what the state church taught. All the girls saw that Angela would not pray for God to curse the missionary's church. They began to notice that she did things differently. Some of the girls began to ask questions during the religion class.

Who are the people who are always singing songs in their meetings?

Who are the people who say that Jesus is coming soon?

Who are the people that keep Sabado, the seventh day?

In answer to those questions, the girls were told, "Oh, those are the ones who worship on the seventh day, Sabado, who CLAIM to believe every word in the Bible. But of course, they do not, because their men wear trousers just like all the other men and their women wear dresses just like all the other women do. It they really followed the Bible they would dress differently. They would wear long flowing robes like people in the Bible times wore. Therefore, you can see that they are not really Bible followers." Then he laughed. Since he laughed, so did all the other girls, except Angela, she just kept quiet.

Angela loved school and she was a hard worker. She was one of the best students. Her grades were always among the highest. She was always on the honor roll. She was a very sweet person and all the other girls, and the teachers liked her. One day the principal called Angela to the office, and she asked, "Angela, are you a member of the church that keeps the seventh day Sabado? Is that why you have always been absent on Sabado?"

Angela answered, "Yes, I am, and that is why I do not come to school on Sabado."

The principal was shocked. "Why you can't be a Sabatista!!!! You are such a good student; you are so intelligent. No person who is as intelligent as you are would ever be a Sabatista. Then the principal tried to appeal to Angela's family loyalty. "What would your father say if he knew you did not worship the way he taught you?"

"Oh, my father knows. He was the first one to learn about the loving God and about His holy Sabado. He is the one who taught me!"

The principal and the teacher had a long talk with Angela, and they tried everything they could to get Angela to admit she had made a mistake by becoming a Sabatista. But Angela would not change her mind. That afternoon was the last time Angela ever went to that school. She went back to the plantation to live with her parents.

But things were not going well for the family on the plantation either. Because Angela's family worshipped on Sabado the people said they were enemies of the state and many of the people did bad things to Angela and her family. One time their whole family got very sick at the same time, and they thought they were all going to die. They were all sick and so extremely sick, they knew someone had poisoned their food. Somehow the family discovered that the last time someone in their family had purchased salt for their own use, the salesperson had put a lot of arsenic into their salt before he closed the little square of paper and made the little bundle which the purchaser took to his/her home when something like salt had been purchased.

It took a long time, but everyone finally got well, except the father. He never did get over the effects of the arsenic poisoning. He was bedridden and he was never able to work again.

Since Angela's father was the family member who worked for the plantation and he could no longer work, the whole family had to leave the plantation. That is when Angela's family moved to the city of Medellin, hoping that the mother and the older children could find jobs to support the family. It was at the church in Medellin where Elsie and her family met Angela's family and learned how badly Angela wanted to go to school.

Elsie remembered how her grandparents had helped her and she had a strong desire to help this young lady. Soon Angela moved into their home and helped Elsie with all the chores, and Lloyd and Elsie helped pay her school tuition. She could also help Elsie shop when she had to go to the market.

Of course, today there are modern stores and markets, and things are quite different but when Lloyd and Elsie went out as missionaries in the early 1940's Medellin, Colombia was much less developed than Canada had been in the early 1940's. In many ways Elsie and Lloyd were true pioneers.

Angela was truly like her name, an angel. She was a hard worker, she was honest, she was very kind, and the whole family loved her. She was such a big help and she studied hard. She became a nurse and after her graduation she, herself became a missionary to several other countries, teaching other people to become nurses. She lived a long, helpful life and always loved Jesus with all her heart.

Lloyd had to be gone visiting other areas very often and his family missed him so much. Sometimes Elsie wondered why it seemed that most of the unique things happened while he was gone. One time while he was gone, she had gone to bed, it was all dark, and she was sound asleep when there was a loud plop on his pillow which was just beside her head. It certainly startled her awake quickly. She turned on the light as soon as she could and there in the middle of his pillow sat a great big, huge frog! Evidently, he had climbed up the wall by using the suction pads on his feet but when he tried to cross the ceiling his weight was too heavy to hold him upside down and he fell right beside Elsie's head. She was thankful he had not landed on her face!

Another time she was alone she had to use the toilet in the middle of the night. She did not want to disturb either of the girls, so she just walked into the bathroom using the streetlight. She carefully sat down on the toilet, and she had barely gotten herself settled when she heard splash, splash, splash. Now what could that be? She jumped up quickly and turned on the bathroom light. There in the toilet swimming around and around was the biggest rat she had ever seen. She quickly flushed the toilet and sent him back to where he had come from. That was the end of Mr. Rat's excursion to her house.

From Colombia, Lloyd was asked to go to Cuba, there they had a one-story house. Elsie and Lloyd's bedroom was at the front of the house, next came his study with his desk and his books, then the bathroom, and behind that the girls' bedroom. Elsie always had her girls take a nap after lunch. She felt it would help to keep them well. One Sabbath afternoon, Lloyd was gone again, Elsie and the girls had eaten their lunch, after lunch was finished, she told them both to go to their room and take a nap. While they slept, she, too would take a nap. Lou went to sleep quickly, Carol did not. Ever since she could remember it had been hard for her to take a nap and now, she felt she was just too old for that baby kind of thing. But she did as she was told and just lay in her bed but could not sleep. Her mind was thinking of all kinds of things she would rather be doing.

Then all of a sudden CRASH! It sounded like it came from the back porch. Behind the girls' bedroom, there was a door separating the rest of the house from a screened-in porch. This porch had a cement sink, the washing machine, a spare room, and a small pantry. Before she could do anything; again, CRASH! Now she was frightened and got out of bed and was going to go see what it was, at the bedroom door she almost bumped into Elsie who was coming quickly back towards the girls' bedroom to see what mischief they were up to now. Before her mother could finish her question of "what are you doing?"

CRASH! CRASH! CRASH! Now they were both a bit frightened and just looked at each other. It sounded like the crashing sounds were coming from the pantry. Then both Elsie and Carol went out to the back the porch and just as Elsie opened the door to the pantry, Carol saw a snake coil back onto a shelf, and again they heard and this time also saw, crash, crash, crash. As it coiled its body around and tried to get to the back of the shelf it was bumping cans and jars from the shelf and onto the tile floor. Well, at least they knew what had made the crashing sounds.

Elsie quickly shut the pantry door and said, "Carol. Go run across the street and call the neighbor man and tell him to come quickly, because we have a snake in the house." There was no phone in their home, so the call for help had to be made in person. This neighbor had a small collection of swords of all different kinds. He grabbed two of them and followed Carol across the street to her home.

Both of the swords were quite long; one was just a regular sword, the other one was a two-edged sword, and both of the edges were jagged because each edge had sharp, curved points sticking out all down its sides. When he got there Elsie explained what had been heard and seen, and he carefully opened the pantry door and then he saw the snake slither to the back of the shelf again. This man struggled for quite some time.

The man would stab the snake with one sword and the snake would try to coil around it and come towards him. Then he would stab it with the other sword and the same thing would happen. The jagged edges of the two-edged sword did not seem to faze the snake in the least.

Finally, the man was able to win and stab the snake close enough to its head so that the snake was not able to keep fighting. When the struggle was over, he took it outside, cut off its head and measured it. That snake was just under five feet long and Elsie never did find out how it had gotten into their house. It was good to have that bit of excitement over and done with!

For Elsie, the hardest part of missionary life in Colombia was not learning how to navigate a market or learn how to live in a new culture. It was not learning a strange language or the hard work that was required of a missionary's wife. It was the many and long absences when Lloyd had to travel to all the distant places which were in his areas of responsibility. He would be gone for several weeks, often for months. There was no telephone in their home, and even if there would have been one, most of the places he went did not have any telephone systems! It would not have helped much if he could have called home, because there was no phone in their home either. Of course, there were no cell phones, no computers, no skype, no means of communication, except written correspondence.

When Lloyd would try to write a letter home he would often arrive home ahead of his letters because there was either no mail service, or if there were any mail service, it was a very primitive mail service where he went. When he left, he was simply GONE until he came home. Elsie and the girls had no idea whether he was safe, what was happening to him, or what he was doing. Before he left, he had told them where he was supposed to go, and when he hoped to be home, but that was all they knew. It was a bit hard and always lonesome.

Sometimes he was able to go in a small plane. Often, he went by "bus." The bus was a large truck onto which someone had put sides and a top. Then boards were put across the inside for the people to sit on. It was not the most comfortable method of travel, but it did get a person from one location to another. The chickens, goats, pigs, produce, luggage, etc. went up on top and as many people as could be crowded in, went inside. If there was not enough room on top of the truck, the people would often hold their chickens or small goats or pigs right on their laps. When he had to go places where there was no plane or the plane didn't go any farther, he would ride the bus, and then when there was no road, he would ride a donkey or just plain use his two legs.

Elsie never complained about these long absences, but she and the girls missed him greatly. After Elsie and Lloyd had both died, Carol found a small notebook of her mother's, in which she had written some of her impressions and experiences. One entry read, "Lloyd is gone, again." That is all it said and that is the only hint she ever gave of how lonesome she was when he was gone so often and for such a long time.

Another interesting entry read, "Mario Camacho has been very sick. Everyone was sure he was going to die. By the grace of God, he actually got well. He then sold one of his two cows and gave the money as a thank offering for being healed. The two cows he owned were his means of earning money to live on because he would take them and go door to door selling their milk." Such love demonstrated for a God of love! When people realize how loving God really is, it changes their lives.

A world war was going on, but Elsie and Lloyd's lives were fairly calm. Yes, there were times when there were local revolutions, and they could look out their upstairs windows towards the main part of town and see buildings burning. These battles were usually political in nature, and Lloyd and Elsie tried hard to stay totally out of all political situations. It is not for missionaries to be involved in the local politics. Their mission is to tell others about Jesus. During the daytime the family was safe. At night everyone had to be off the streets and home by curfew and were safe as long as no one went out until after the curfew was lifted the next morning.

One time Lloyd had a meeting to go to and he had to get dressed quickly and in the dark, and he didn't realize until later during the day that in the darkness he had put on one black shoe and one brown shoe. He just hoped that not too many people had noticed.

Lloyd and Elsie were finally able to get a car (small by today's standards) it had been ordered and then sent to them from America. It came by boat and when it arrived there was a lot of excitement. It made quite a change in their lives. It made it so much easier for Lloyd to visit the schools and churches which were closer to where they lived, and which was all a part of his regular work.

For example, Lloyd was in midst of helping to establish a high school/junior college a few miles outside of the town in which Lloyd's office was located and where they lived. If you rode the bus out to the school site, the bus line stopped two miles from the school, and you had to walk the last two miles whether it was sunny and warm or raining. The people who lived along this road were not always the friendliest and it was challenging at times. With a car you could drive easily down that road, turn and go through the school gate, right onto the property. When Elsie had to go to the market, she did not have to struggle on to the bus with their heavy bolsas full of groceries. Another advantage to having their own car was being able to drive right to the churches in town rather than ride the bus and then have to walk blocks through sometimes unfriendly areas of town. The car made a lot of things easier for them.

Chapter Eight

One evening when Lloyd came home from the office, he announced to the family that he had to go on another trip, quite an extended one this time. Before anyone could comment on that announcement, he added, "But this trip will be different because I am going to go by car, and you are all going to go along with me." Then what happiness and excitement there was in their little home.

There was much excitement for the girls and much talking, planning, and work for Lloyd and Elsie. The family was going to leave the city of Medellin and cross over the Andes Mountains and go all the way to the center of Venezuela. There Lloyd was planning to hold the first ever "junior" camp for the whole union. It was actually more of a "youth" camp because there had never been such a thing as a "junior camp" in that area ever before. Lloyd decided to begin with the young people who were a little bit older, just as he had done in Canada.

Lloyd was planning to hold meetings in many places along the way. He had to take all his supplies. Elsie had to take their own bedding, their own hammocks to sleep in, clothes for hot weather and clothes for cold weather, dishes and utensils to eat with, a small camp stove so she could fix their meals, a few kettles, and some food. Some food would be able to be purchased in the local villages if their arrival happened to coincide with the local market day.

Finally, everything was ready, and it came time to load the car and begin their journey. Lloyd was a very good packer, and the car had a good trunk, so he was able to squeeze everything into the car. It was very full but there was room for all of them. So, everyone got into the car and away they went. At first the road was paved, then after a while it was just gravel. Away from the cities, the road was usually gravel and narrow, most places just wide enough for one lane. In the plains there were usually places to turn out if you met an on-coming vehicle. In the mountainous areas, which was a lot of the time, there were some turnouts in case you met another vehicle coming towards you. The vehicle coming down had to back up because it was steep, and it would have been harder for the vehicle going up.

The little car went up the mountain and down the mountain, then up another one. Day after day the family went up and down, but there were lots of interesting things to see. Sometimes they drove right under small waterfalls. Other times the water just came down the mountain and ran across the road and Lloyd had to drive right through it. Many times, their journey took them up so high that no trees were growing, just short scrubby bushes. It was very cold. The few animals that lived there had thick, bushy long fur, and the people who lived there had to struggle to stay warm. Often, the car was so high up in the mountains that one could look down on the clouds. Carol liked to stick her hand out the window and think she was holding a cloud, well at least touching one. Then at times their journey took them down where it was quite warm, and they would go into and out of the jungle. This was all new and interesting to Elsie and the girls, Lloyd had been to many of these places on his previous travels.

The family would stop in a little village where Lloyd knew there were some people who loved and served God. Then he would stay there a day or sometimes two and hold meetings for them. The local people were so glad to have someone visit them. Sometimes he would have weddings and baptisms because these people were so far away from larger towns that there was no regular minister. So, the people had saved these occasions until a minister would come to visit them.

These were indigenous people, and the Indians had lovely straight black hair and reddish-brown skin. Often Elsie was only the second white lady that these folks had ever seen, and the girls were the very first white children that the people had ever seen. The indigenous people were as curious about their visitors as the missionary family was about them. Carol had very curly white-blond hair and the people would feel it, touch it, and rub it between their fingers and ask how it got that way! The people would rub the girls' arms to see what color these strange-looking girls were under their light skin.

If the church happened to have real benches, sometimes Elsie's family would be able to sleep on the benches in the small church. If there were no benches, just boards between two supports, these were too narrow to sleep on and the family would sleep outside. Lloyd and Elsie would put up their hammocks and sleep outdoors. When they slept in their hammocks, Lloyd would always try to find three trees close enough together so that he could tie their hammocks close together. He would tie his hammock between two trees. Then he would tie one end of Elsie's hammock onto the same tree where he had tied his hammock. He would tie the other end of her hammock to the third tree. That way they could have their heads as close together as possible. The girls would sleep in the car, one on the front seat and one on the back seat.

These were service hammocks, not fancy relaxing hammocks like most people have now days. The hammocks were woven of heavy cords, so were very sturdy and strong. The length was about the same as the hammocks we have today, but these were very wide. If you sat sideways in them, you could just let your legs hang down and it was like sitting in a swing or you could extend your legs right out in front of you, and also lean you head and back against the other side, so it was just like people sit in recliners today to relax. When it was time to sleep, the person would lie lengthwise, and the hammock was so wide that the occupant would wrap one side around over the top of them and then wrap the other side around on top of the first side. It was just like being in a cocoon, and it helped to keep them warm when the nights were cold.

One night everyone was sleeping soundly, Lloyd and Elsie in their hammocks and the girls in the car, when Lloyd felt his hammock go jiggle, jiggle, jiggle. He woke up very quickly as he didn't know whether it was a person or an animal. He laid very still and quiet, and he listened as hard as he could to hear if anything or anyone was moving around close to the hammocks or in the bushes close by. He didn't hear anything or anyone. As he was lying there, pretty soon he felt jiggle, jiggle, jiggle again, only this time it was a bit stronger. What could it be? Again, he was quiet and still and listened as hard as he could, but he still could not hear anything or anyone moving, either in the bushes or close to the hammocks. But soon, jiggle, jiggle, jerk, jiggle even harder than before, so he knew he had to do something. He called out, "Elsie, are you okay?" Right away her answer came back to him, "No, I'm not, I tried to change the position I was sleeping in, and my hammock went upside down. I'm upside down and can't get right side up again." Now that Lloyd knew what was happening, he got right up and turned her hammock over, so she was sleeping on her back again. Then the two of them had a good sleep the rest of the night. Years later this provided them many laughs.

One morning it was time to move on to the next town. Lloyd had finished his meetings the night before, and he had a schedule to keep. Several weeks before he had left on this trip, he had written to the people and sent them his schedule so all the people could be advised that he was coming and would be at the town nearest to them on such and such a day at a certain time. This was definitely not a vacation, but a lot of work. And the family had to be where it was scheduled for them to be when they were supposed to be there because the people would be waiting for them and many of these folks had to walk a long distance to arrive at the meeting place on time and at the appointed day.

The mountains were steep, and Lloyd had been having trouble with the car. One time a small fire had started in the engine and Lloyd and Elsie had to jump out and throw some dirt on it to put it out. Since the roads were dirt, it was easy to find dirt!

One day around noon time Lloyd had just driven through a small village and was ready to start up another mountain. He had just gotten to the edge of the village when he arrived at a bar across the road. Of course, he had to stop. There was a small building at the side of the road and a guard with a large gun came out to talk to them.

"Where are you going?" he asked. Lloyd told him the name of the town they needed to visit, which was on the other side of the mountain.

"Why you cannot go there!"

"Oh, but I must. The people are expecting me tomorrow night, those folks are all waiting for me. There is no phone access to them so there is no way I could let them know I could not get there. This has been planned for many weeks. I must go now to arrive where and when I told them I would."

"No, you cannot go now, there is no way you would be able to get to the top of the mountain and down the other side before dark. The bandits are too active right now and you would not be safe. You are foreigners in my country. And if you were killed, your country would not be happy with my country. There is no possibility of your going. You may not go and that is final."

Lloyd was a good talker, and he really talked this time. He knew it was his duty to be at that town the next evening. He argued a bit with the soldier and finally the soldier said, "Well, you may go, but it is against my command. If something happens to you it is not my country's fault. It is your own responsibility; we cannot be responsible for what happens to you. Just keep driving and do not stop for anything."

Lloyd and Elsie talked it over, prayed about it, and decided to go on up the mountain. The little missionary family went up, and up, and up some more. The road was very narrow and so steep. Sometimes large rocks would fall down the mountain side and land in the middle of the road. Sometimes the bandits would roll a large rock out into the middle of the road. Therefore, when a truck, bus, or car came around a corner and there was a huge rock in the road, the people never knew whether it had just rolled down the mountain or whether the bandits had put it there and were hiding, just waiting to rob whoever stopped to remove the rock from the road. It made traveling quite an adventure.

As Lloyd drove along, the road went higher and higher up into the mountain. The family saw fewer and fewer people. The road was so steep and narrow and had many tight hairpin switchbacks. These switchbacks were so narrow and sharp that Lloyd had to drive very carefully. Any trucks or buses which came to these switchbacks had to go very slowly, move forward a little, then back up and go forward a bit more, often backing up three times. Too often they misjudged, and the bus or truck went off the road and tumbled down the mountain, killing many people. Sometimes the switchbacks were even frightening to the family in their little car.

After a while they were so high into the mountain that there were no more trees growing. It was a bit foggy and cloudy, so their journey took them in and out of the clouds. Every now and then there was a small stream which flowed down the mountain side. Sometimes Lloyd would drive under it, so it was like going under a waterfall. Other times he just splashed through it on the road. The girls thought it was great fun.

At one point the car started to go sputter, sputter, spit, spit and Lloyd said, "Oh, no, the engine is really getting hot. But we are so close to the top, if we can make it that far we should be able to make it down the other side okay because going down will be much easier on the car."

Lloyd was able to drive on a little more, he went around another corner and the poor car went sputter, sputter, sputter. Then Lloyd said, "It just won't go any more. The engine is too hot, and we must put some more water in the radiator. The water should help cool it down and then I think we could make it to the top. Going down the other side will be much easier as the engine won't have to work so hard going down."

Now what? Lloyd had been told not to stop or get out of the car, but to keep moving as quickly as he could. Elsie had a bit of drinking water which had been boiled so it was safe to drink, but Lloyd could not waste it on the car. He had just driven past a small waterfall around the last corner. Elsie had some small kettles which she used for cooking and Lloyd decided that he and Elsie would each take two containers and go back around the corner and fill them with water. By the time they got back to the car it would have cooled down enough that he could add the cold water to the radiator.

Lloyd and Elsie specifically said, "Girls, stay in the car, be sure to lock all the doors, and do not talk to anyone." Talk to anyone? Nobody had even seen anyone for a long time! The two little girls did as they were told: they locked the doors and then they knelt on the back seat and watched out the back window as Daddy and Mama walked away from them and down the same road which Daddy had just driven up. Soon the parents went around the bend, and the girls could not see them anymore. Now what could the girls do?

The girls wiggled and bounced and talked and then they began to get a little scared. What if Mama and Daddy didn't come back? Both the girls had understood what the soldier had told Lloyd about the bandits on the mountain. As there was nothing else to do, Carol began to look around outside a little more carefully. On the right side of the road, the mountain went straight up from the edge of the road. On the left side, there was a very narrow bit of land right beside the road before it dropped sharply down, down, and down. Since it was only a one lane road this was probably used as a turn out in case you met an on-coming vehicle. That was not as interesting as what she noticed on that little narrow strip of land. Right beside the road on that small space was a very small fire, and it was burning!

Yes, it is natural for fires to burn. But way up high in the mountains where trees don't grow, firewood is very scarce and often people must use animal dung as the fuel for their fires. No one builds a fire unless it is absolutely necessary to cook something to eat or to try to warm themselves and the fire is only made as small as necessary to complete their task. Once there is a fire burning, the person or persons certainly do not go away and leave it burning! That would be a terrible waste their precious fuel. If there is a fire burning, there must be people there. The family had not seen any people and besides that they knew that the only people up there at this time were the bandits.

Then the girls saw Daddy and Mama coming back around the bend with their containers full of water. The engine had had a little time to cool down while the parents were gone so as soon as they got back to the car Daddy put the water into the radiator as quickly as he could while Mama put the containers away. Then Daddy got into the car and tried to start it. It started up right away and he drove away as quickly as possible.

There are two important things to know about being so high up in the mountains. It is very quiet, and a person can hear any noise from a long distance away. The bandits had plenty of time to hear any vehicle coming and get ready to attack. The other is that with fuel so precious no one runs away and leaves a fire burning. Did this missionary family's angels make a lot of noise as Daddy came driving up the mountain so that the bandits got scared thinking someone was pursuing them, and the bandits had run away to hide leaving their precious fire? Another possibility was, did the angels close the eyes and ears of the bandits so that they did not hear or see the family's car? This is one secret no one would ever know this side of heaven.

Since Lloyd had almost reached the pass at the top of that mountain, he crossed the pass and began the descent down the other side. In that part of the world, the sun sets quite early, and it begins to get dark as soon as the sun sets. Their car had good lights, so Lloyd just kept driving. It was a bit late and completely dark by the time he reached the bottom of that mountain. There was another little house beside the road and another big barricade bar across the whole road. Of course, he had to stop and the guard with his gun came out of the little guard house. The guard was very surprised to see the car and the family!

Before the guard lifted the bar, he asked in a rather startled and unbelieving voice, "Where did you come from?"

Lloyd answered, giving him the name of the little town at the base on the other side of the mountain, which they had left that afternoon.

"Oh, but that's impossible! No one has been over the mountain all day. Just yesterday a car and a bus tried to cross over. The bandits stopped the car, robbed, and then killed all the people in the car. When the bus came along, the bandits also stopped it and robbed and killed everyone on the bus. No one can cross that mountain at this time. It is night, it is dark, you couldn't have come over that mountain safely."

He was still shaking his head when he lifted the bar and let the family go on their way.

When God's people are doing the work He wants them to do, He will send His angels to protect them. He certainly protected this little missionary family on that day.

The family was not always at the top of the mountains. Much of the time they were down a bit lower where there were lots of trees and bushes. There were not many people, but a few people lived scattered around in these isolated areas. The road was not any better nor any wider and it took them a long time to get where they were going. Often Lloyd could not go faster than fifteen miles an hour. But at least he was making forward progress. The girls sat in the back amusing themselves as best they could, as they just rode all day long, day after day. At fifteen miles per hour, it takes a long time to go a short distance.

At noon Lloyd would try to find one of the few wider spaces at the side of the road, one where they could not see any houses, and they couldn't see any people. Then he would pull over and get out the little camp stove. Elsie would get out a kettle and prepare some hot food for the four of them. Other times they just had sandwiches. But it was a little bit of time where the girls could get out, stretch their legs, run around a bit, and get rid of the feeling of sitting still and riding all day.

Something interesting usually happened. It seemed like no matter where Lloyd stopped the bushes grew people! Even if they didn't see houses, soon there were boys and girls climbing up the mountain side from down below or scrambling down from somewhere up higher. The boys and girls weren't the only ones; the mamas, aunts, and grandparents all came to get a peek at these foreigners stopping in their region for a bite to eat. The foreigners looked so different, and their food was sometimes different. This pale missionary family were a novelty for the people living there. Often the men would also come, each man always carried his long machete at his side.

The machete was a long, wide-bladed knife with a very sharp cutting edge The machetes were a very handy tool for the men. The men used these knives for many purposes. The machetes were used to cut long grasses to be used as bedding for their animals, also to harvest food for their families and the animals, they cut sugar cane, bushes, and small trees, and chopped wood to be used as fuel. Sometimes the machetes were used by the men to kill snakes and sometimes the chickens, goats or other animals which they used for food. The men even used their machetes to settle disputes between people, settling a dispute by this manner usually resulted with the loser often losing his head.

All the indigenous people were very curious. They would talk amongst themselves and giggle and laugh. These people were not bashful as they watched the picnicking family, the family likewise watched them back!

Some would get bolder and come to talk with Elsie's family. The local people were always full of questions, and the family enjoyed talking with them and answering their questions. The family sort of got used to having an audience while they ate. As the family finished eating, they often shared something with the boys and girls standing around. No one could share anything with the kids at the beginning of the meal or there would soon have been too many folks wanting food, and Elsie did not have room to bring that much extra food with them. If she happened to have used a tin can that day, the people always wanted the empty can! It was considered a real treasure to have a tin can which could be used for carrying something in, to dip water from the stream with, or to just use for storage.

One day while Elsie's family was sitting at the side of the road eating, the usual group of interested onlookers had gathered around them. The group was friendly and stood there watching them eat. The onlookers also had some questions for them, "Where are you going? What are you doing? Can you give us some of your food?" As the family were finishing their meal, they shared a little bit of something with the children. When the meal was finished and the usual sharing was done, Elsie began to pack up the kettles and dishes, and got ready to put things away. The girls were busy enjoying running around a bit longer and not sitting in the car.

It seems like Lloyd had been watching the road while Elsie and the girls were getting ready to leave. He had noticed that a group of four or five men were coming down the road towards them. Each man had the normal machete hanging from his waist. These men paused a short distance away from the family and began to talk amongst themselves.

Soon one of the men came walking towards the car, presumably to talk with Lloyd. As the man got closer to Lloyd, he stopped, then he suddenly turned around and walked back to his group of men and the men began to talk together again. This group was just far enough away so that neither Elsie, Lloyd nor the girls could hear what the men were saying. Very soon a different one of the men came walking back to where the family was preparing to leave. When this man got close to them, he also suddenly stopped, turned around and walked toward his group and they began to talk amongst themselves again. Then a different man came towards the family, but the same thing happened as had happened with the other men who tried to come closer to the family.

All of a sudden Lloyd said very firmly, "Girls, get in the car NOW, do it quickly, and lock the doors!" When your daddy talks that way and in that tone of voice, you do not question anything, you just do it! Then he told Elsie to just throw her things into the car and get in and lock her door. In those days, early 1940's, the cars did not have automatic locks as they do today. Each door had a little knob and had to be locked individually by pushing the little knob downwards. While Elsie and the girls were getting into the car, Lloyd hurried around to his side, got in, started the car, and they drove away as quickly as possible. That was a rather interesting but strange experience.

They continued safely on with their journey and Lloyd held many successful meetings, a very fun "junior" camp, and they all enjoyed a safe trip home.

When they got home, Lloyd continued with his regular work routine. Several months later Lloyd was asked to go and visit some of the same places where they had travelled through on their way to the "junior" camp. One evening he was holding a meeting in one of the small towns. After the meeting was over, he was talking with the people as they left, and he noticed one man who hung back a bit. After most of the people had gone this man came up to Lloyd and said, "Pastor Lloyd, were you here a few months ago with your family?"

Lloyd answered, "yes we were."

The man continued asking, "Do you remember stopping alongside of the road to eat one day at noon?"

"Yes, that was our habit."

"Would you please answer a question for me?"

"I'd be happy to, if I can."

"Who were those tall men that you had with you? They were white men, like you, these men were dressed in clothes just like you wore, except their clothes were all white."

"Why we had no one with us. It was just me, my wife, and our two little girls."

Lloyd's car was not very big. The four of them could fit nicely into it and if everyone squeezed together closely, it may have been possible to have gotten one more adult in with them, but certainly not four big, tall men.

Then the man continued, "Oh, no, you had some very tall men with you. Those men were white skinned like you are, and their clothes were like yours except their clothes were all white.

Then Lloyd knew for sure, and he said, "Those men were our guardian angels. We always ask God to send His angels with us to protect us when we travel."

"On, no, those men were not angels. They did not look at all like angels. Those men were white men just like you are, only those men were much taller than you are, and their clothes were all white even though their clothes looked like yours did."

Now Lloyd had to explain to the man that our angels do not always look like we think angels should look. God's angels can look just like ordinary people, but nevertheless they are God's angels sent to protect us.

Then the man told Lloyd this story. "My friends and I were going to kill all of you that day. We were going to kill you with our machetes, burn your bodies, and take your car. That was our plan, but every time one of us would start to walk towards you, one of those very tall white men would step in front of you or whoever we walked towards and there was nothing we could do. We just had to turn around and leave you alone. Several of us tried several times and always one of those tall white men, dressed in white, would step in front of you to protect you and none of us could get close to you."

Elsie's family had never seen their guardian angels that day. However, those men who came to do them harm saw those angels clearly. God is so good to have let Lloyd meet one of the men who saw his family's angels so that man could tell him firsthand what he had seen. And the rest of the family could know about one of the many times God provided His special protection over them! Many times, God's angels protect His people, and the people never know there was a visible angel right beside them.

The youth/junior camp that Lloyd held in Venezuela was a lot of fun for everyone who was there. It was very different than the junior camps where children and youth can go today. Elsie and Lloyd slept in their hammocks; the girls slept in the car. By now everyone was rather used to that arrangement.

There was a large "building" on the grounds. It had a cement floor, and posts held up a corrugated tin roof. All around the outside it had wooden walls that went halfway up, then it was just open to the air and sky. The girls who attended as campers tied their hammocks to the posts that held up the roof and the boys slept outside on the ground. A small group of the boys climbed a tall tree and built a rough platform, and they slept up there.

In this building were tables which had benches at them and that is where all of the campers ate their meals. Elsie's family also ate their meals in that "building" with the rest of the campers. That building was also used for many other activities such as worships, games, and talks. Every morning the girl campers would sit at some of the tables and sort big piles of rice, removing small stones, bugs, and dirt. Then they did the same with big piles of beans. It was a lot of work to prepare all this food for everyone. But all the girls laughed and talked so it was even fun doing that work.

There were an interesting variety of tasty local foods that the missionary family had learned to eat and enjoy. While at camp, for the morning meal the campers and the family had beans and rice, at noon they had rice and beans, then in the evening they had beans and rice again. Sometimes the camp personnel were able to purchase a bit of fruit for the morning meal. All the campers enjoyed the meals because that is what they ate at home---it was simple, but it was good, and it was nourishing. Therefore, everyone enjoyed eating it together with their new friends.

Big pans of water were placed outside, and everyone had to wash his own dishes, but this too, was done with a lot of laughter.

While the girls cleaned the rice and beans, some of the larger young men would make several trips down to the river and carry barrels of water back to camp. This was used to cook, wash dishes, drink, and shower.

The showers were another fascinating experience for the missionary family. Someone put four poles into the ground and then burlap was nailed to the posts on four sides, with a make-shift door on one side. There was no roof, just sunshine and sky. The boys would place a large barrel of water on the ground inside of the "shelter" and when you wanted to take a shower you went in there, dipped a tin cup into the water, and then poured the water over you. It was all very efficient. There was a shower for the girls on one side of the camp and another for the boys on the other side. Everyone was happy to be able to be so clean and no one had to go and wash in the river!

One day the boys were quite late with bringing the water up from the river. When the boys got to camp, they explained that there had been a very large snake in the path, and it was not possible for them to pass until the snake had safely gone on its way.

The toilet was another interesting building. It was built at the edge of the camp and was like an outhouse but only closed in on two sides and the back. The front was all open. It faced out over a large valley which had several mountain ranges on the other side of it. It was a very beautiful sight to sit and be able to look out for such a large distance and see so many natural beauties.

One evening the girls had a bit of excitement. They were all sound asleep when suddenly one of the girls screamed. Of course, when she screamed, the commotion awoke all the rest of the girls, and they began to scream in sympathy with the first girl. They were not sure what they were screaming about but since one screamed, they all screamed. A large cow had gotten into the "building" where they were sleeping and stuck her face into the hammock of one of the girls. Being wide awake now, the girls noticed that several cows had somehow pushed open the small gate that served as a door, or maybe someone forgot to close it properly the evening before. At any rate, the cows were curious about these new creatures hanging from the posts, so the cows just had to investigate. Soon the cows were shooed back outside, the gate securely shut, and everyone went back to their hammocks and to sleep.

Next morning there was a lot of teasing by the boys about the girls being so scared of just plain old ordinary cows.

All of the campers had a thoroughly good time. Many had made new friends, and all were anxious to know when the next camp would be held. Lloyd was happy to know it had been such a success. Everyone began to prepare for their journeys to their own homes, many planning on coming to the next camp.

When camp was over Lloyd packed the car in preparation for going home. Then Elsie, Lloyd, and the girls started their journey home. For some reason, Lloyd wore his camp director's uniform that day. He did not usually do that as it was reserved for special occasions. Maybe he was in a hurry to get on the road towards home since they had such a long way to go, or maybe he had been wearing one all week and it was just convenient to keep it on, or maybe all his other clothes were dirty! They drove down the road a little while and soon came to a very long line of cars. All the cars were just stopped and were waiting for who knows what.

After they sat there waiting for a while, a soldier with his gun came walking back past all the cars. When he got to their car, he greeted Lloyd, who by now spoke Spanish like a native. He took one look at Lloyd in his uniform and immediately presumed that Lloyd was some important military man. He spoke very respectfully, and he said, "Sir come follow me, you do not need to sit and wait in this long line." Lloyd was happy to oblige and pulled out of the line and went right past that huge, long line of cars. The soldiers were having some type of military inspection that day and the family was just waved right on through. Was this another time that God impressed Lloyd to leave his uniform on so that their family did not have to go through the inspection and get into who knows what trouble for being in that area at that time. They were still considered heretics and undesirables in that part of the country.

Chapter Nine

During her adult years, Elsie sent birthday cards to Papa and New Mama, she wrote letters to them talking about some of her experiences. But she never received any answers. One day a letter did arrive from New Mama. What a surprise! The first time any communication had come from her to Elsie and her family.

New Mama's youngest daughter was getting married, she was the first of New Mama's children to get married, and New Mama wanted Lloyd to perform the wedding ceremony for them. To think that New Mama actually wanted Lloyd to come and do this favor for them when she had forbidden him to even come onto their property in the past was a real change in attitude. She signed the letter, "from home."

Elsie was totally shocked! With tears in her eyes she said, "Those two words, 'from home' are the most loving thing she has ever said to me."

Lloyd and Elsie were living on a minister's salary, she was not working for a salary, and their two children were in church school. That request from New Mama was something they could ill afford. It would mean a long trip with all the expenses involved in taking a family of four that far. Lloyd was working in Miami, Florida at that time and it would mean a drive to mid-western Canada, but they talked it over and decided they should honor that request. This was just another example of how Lloyd and Elsie always sacrificed to do for others, when they could not afford to do for themselves. The trip was made, the wedding celebrated, but nothing more was said "from home."

A few years passed and Carol was to be married. Elsie wanted her Papa to come to the wedding of his first granddaughter. Again, New Mama said that he was too busy, it was impossible for them afford the trip for him (just one person) to go from mid-western Canada all the way down to Miami, Florida! She would not allow him to come. Just another time Elsie had to celebrate an important occasion without her Papa.

Three years later Carol's first daughter was born, Papa's first great grandchild. When the baby was 6 months old, Elsie's youngest daughter, Carol's sister, was to graduate from college. Everyone would be there. This time Papa finally put his foot down. He was going to go, by himself, see his second granddaughter graduate from college as a nurse, and he wanted to see his first great grandchild. He did come. And how much he enjoyed the trip and being with his daughter and her two daughters, and his first great grandchild. There were four generations of Papa's family there and he was so very happy to be with them all. It was a peaceful, fun, and loving time. That was the only time he was able to visit Elsie, his oldest daughter, and be with her family away from the farm.

During all the years, Elsie had not been idle. She helped Lloyd whenever and wherever she could. She loved children! And in so many countries where they had lived, there was not much, if anything, done for the children. So that became her fervent goal.

She was able to accompany Lloyd on some of his trips and she always held Sabbath school workshops for the people. Both men and women were so eager to learn and so happy for the instruction Elsie shared with them.

At that time the children's Sabbath school lessons were on a three-year cycle, so she got busy and wrote three books, one for each year. She made a whole Sabbath school program for those of kindergarten age, a program for each Sabbath of the year. She included the lesson for the day, songs and the music for the songs, stories, and finger plays, all to coincide with the day's lesson. She also included ideas for visual aids and the directions on how to make them. She wrote the books in English and then she translated them into Spanish. She also translated many of the English songs into Spanish. The books were so greatly appreciated by the people, who up until then had had nothing special for their children's programs.

Whenever she held a workshop, she would have samples to show the people, things they could make themselves, things they could afford because in many of the countries the people were quite poor.

She demonstrated what a sand box was, and how you could make the story more interesting for the children by having little paper figures to move around in the sand to illustrate the Bible lesson. Of course, most of the people could not afford to buy or make a sand box or the little tables which they went into. She could not travel with a little table and sand box either, but she made do by putting dirt into a flat cardboard box.

She always tried to adapt her illustrations to what was available in the country she was in and to the financial recourses of the people who lived there. One of the countries they visited was Guatemala. While she was in Guatemala, holding a Sabbath school workshop she demonstrated the idea of some type of "sand box" and the little paper, "people" that could be made to demonstrate the Bible lesson. The people there were so happy for the ideas and the instruction she gave them that the next day several of them came to her with little "people" which they had made from sticks. The people could not even afford the paper and crayons to make cutouts, but they had good imaginations and innovatively used what they had.

The people found a little stick, of the desired size; then took scraps of cloth to dress their "person." It was very easy to obtain sticks in their yards or the jungle around their homes and most of the women made their own clothes and nothing was wasted, so all the women had small scraps of cloth available. The women took non patterned fabric and bunched it up to form a head for their "person." Then with a pencil the people drew faces on their miniature "people" and then the women cut locks of their own hair to make hair for their "people." These tufts of hair were then sewed by hand onto their little "people's" heads. All this work was done by hand and the little "people" were so cute. These little figurines were like miniature dolls.

So, it turned out that the little girl who was told, "you are too dumb and too stupid to learn anything" grew up to be a big help to so many people. She even wrote three books in two languages. Always she tried to bring honor and glory to the God she loved so much. Many years later, when Carol's children were all grown and living away from home, Carol was able to go with her husband to several countries around the world and she saw people still using her mother's books and the ideas in them!

During these busy years of ministry, Lloyd still had to travel a lot. One year the General Conference asked Elsie to be in charge of the kindergarten department at the General Conference session which was to be held in San Francisco that year. She did not feel worthy of this, but as her custom was, she believed that if God asked her to do something she should try to do it. She prayed much for God's help and with His help she did accomplish the fact. She had 500 children in each of her programs at that large meeting. She had a program every day, morning and evening, and then special weekend meetings for the kindergarten children.

Epilogue

The "ugly old turkey egg" turned out not to be ugly after all. She was a very nice-looking lady, and most importantly she had a very beautiful Christian character. She was always very humble and helpful to everyone who needed help.

Two rather interesting events happened in Elsie's life. One helped to shape the type of person she was and the other showed what type of person she really was. When she was a young new wife, she went to a large meeting of the conference with Lloyd. There the gentlemen had a lovely display of the latest books for sale. Elsie had always loved to read, and now she had a few pennies with which to buy a book. She did love books. She carefully chose her book and timidly stood in line waiting to pay for it. As she was waiting an older woman came elbowing her way in front of everyone and in a rather loud voice said, "I am Mrs. President Elder So-and-So, take me first." Elsie decided right then and there that **IF** her husband was ever an important someone, she would never push herself in front of anyone else.

The second event happened after Lloyd had been a minister for quite some time and was in administrative work, he was invited to be the president of the Greater New York Conference. The three languages he spoke fluently would be a big help in that large city with so many diverse cultures. It so happened that Lloyd and Elsie arrived in New York shortly before the yearly camp meeting started so the two of them had not had much opportunity to get to know many of the people in that area, nor had the people had opportunity to get acquainted with them. While in the early days of camp meeting Elsie went into the kitchen just to see if there was anything she could do to help. She was always so helpful and humble. The matron looked askance at her and didn't recognize her, so she said, "yes, there are a pile of pans from last night that have burnt-on crust on them. You may clean those for me."

Elsie said, "I'll be happy to help" and then went to work with vigor to clean the ugly pots and pans. She had had plenty of experience scrubbing burned stuck-on food from pans. She was facing the sink and scrubbing hard, but after a while someone else came into the kitchen and Elsie overheard this new lady say to the matron, "do you know who that is over there?" "No," answered the matron. "Well, she is the new conference president's wife. You should not allow her to do that filthy job."

Soon the matron came over to Elsie and said you've done enough we'll find something else for you to do. But Elsie just smiled at her and finished the job she had been assigned to do.

This lovely lady, Elsie was my mother. She always had to live very frugally. But she and my dad, Lloyd, always lived by the principle of being very generous and giving liberally and sacrificially to help others. They always thought of others first and each of them helped so many people spiritually, physically, and financially, even when it meant that they, themselves had to do without to give to others.

With God's help she was able to bring the experience of God's love to many children and adults around the world., both by word and by her example.

Even though my mother was so young when her mama died, she remembered the lessons that Papa and Mama had taught her about always loving Jesus and being kind to others. Was she perfect? No, none of us have reached that state yet. But she was always kind and thoughtful. She did the best she could with the many physical, mental, and emotional scars which she carried all of her life, and she was a very loving and good mother!

Until she died at over 92 years of age, whenever I would ask her about her childhood with New Mama, she would burst into tears and say, "I just can't talk about that. I've tried so hard to put it all behind me and try to totally forgive her."

The few examples of abuse that I have given I've mostly learned from others who were adults when Elsie was growing up. The lady who came to take care of New Mama so that Elsie could go back to school when New Mama's first baby was born, was one of those people. She shared her own experience by telling me about that situation. After my parents retired, they lived in Mesa, Arizona for many years and my husband and I lived there also. This lady came up to me after a church potluck and told me that story.

One of New Mama's brothers was another one who shared these experiences with me, as did some others who had lived in that small community while Elsie was a child. Many of these people had retired to Mesa, Arizona, some at least for the winter months. These are the ones who came up to me and volunteered their experiences and expressed their sorrow that they had not been able to help relieve her sufferings.

The summer of my parents' 65th wedding anniversary, my sister and I and our husbands accompanied our parents on a trip to Canada. We were able to visit the little country church where Elsie and her own Mama and Papa had attended. There we learned other things. My Uncle Archie had rented a van so the eight of us could all ride together and as we drove along, I over-heard some of their conversations. At that time Uncle Archie told his experience about the guitar. The stories about the chewing gum and the orange peels also slipped out at that time.

One winter my husband and I were vacationing in Mexico. At that time, Aunt Melvina and her husband happened to be there at the same time as we were. It was her birthday, so we got her a cake and some balloons. She was so overwhelmed. She had tears in her eyes when she said, "this is the very first time in my whole life that I ever had a balloon!" Those poor abused children had nothing, yet as adults, they all had cheerful attitudes and were always so helpful to others.

Elsie and her siblings, Archie and Melvina did not express anger or resentment about their childhood. Yes, there was a lot of pain, heart ache and sad memories, but not one of them showed vengeance to anyone of New Mama's family.

Most importantly, my mother, Elsie, always loved and served her loving Savior and that is the way she was able to overcome the ashes and brokenness in her life.

Only two names have been altered in this story, all other names are the real names of the people involved. In the parts of this story which occurred in Canada, or the United States of America, Mama and Papa are always Lydia and Chris, Elsie's loving parents. New Mama was Chris's second wife, I have not used her name or the names of her three children as some of their relatives are still living and I do not want to do anything to hurt any of them. Mother and Dad always refer to Lloyd's parents, Sam and Lydia. The words mama, papa, dad, mother, etc. used in the stories about people in other countries refer to the families involved in their part of the story.

"… to comfort all who mourn; … to give them beauty for ashes, the oil of joy for mourning, the garment of praise for the spirit of heaviness… that He may be glorified." Isaiah 61:2b, 3 NKJV

Truly, Elsie's, my mother's, life has demonstrated this Bible text in many ways. She was cheerful, she was happy, she loved others, she gave her time, her money, her talent of writing children's books and dedicated her whole life to helping others. By her life she glorified the God she loved. I have written down these few details, hoping that they also will glorify Him. **God is LOVE!**

Useful References

In case you are interested in looking further into the reasons why my grandfather, Samuel and my father Lloyd were so dedicated to sharing God's love and the truth about the seventh-day Sabbath I have listed a few references which can help your search.

Cruden's Complete Concordance of the Old and New Testaments. By Alexander Cruden, A.M published by Zondervan.

Young's Analytical Concordance to the Bible. By Robert Young, LL.D., published by MacDonald Publishing Company.

- When using a concordance to find information about a certain subject it is helpful to know that the concordances usually are divided into references as to whether a word is a noun or a verb. Examples could be such as:
- Jake eats (v) eats(n). The verb "eats" means to consume food, the noun "eats" means the food to be, or which is eaten.
- Black spots (n or v) the noun means marks made by something black, the v means the act of spotting or making something else partially black.

You may also use the publications of the Roman Catholic Church. These are written by Catholic dignitaries. I do not believe that humans should be called "Reverend" because that is a name pertaining to God alone, but some of these men have given themselves these titles so I have used that title here.

A Doctrinal Catechism, by Rev. Stephen Keenan, p.74

Rev. Dr. Butler's Catechism, Revised, p. 57

Plain Talk About the Protestantism of Today, by Msgr. Segur, p.213.

....A History of the Councils of the Church: from the Original Documents, by Rev. Charles Joseph Hefele, D.D., Bishop of Rottenburg, book 6, sec. 93, canon 29 (vol 11, p. 316

It is also interesting to study the history of how we arrived at the names we give to the days in our week.

Name God Gave	Latin Name	Saxon Name	English Name	Spanish Name
First Day Gen 1:5	Dies Solis	Sun's Day	Sunday	Domingo
Second Day Gen 1:8	Dies Lunae	Moon's Day	Monday	Lunes
Third Day Gen 1:13	Dies Martis	Tiw's Day	Tuesday	Martes
Fourth Day Gen 1:19	Dies Mercurii	Woden's Day	Wednesday	Miercoles
Fifth Day Gen 1:23	Diew Jovis	Thor's Day	Thursday	Jueves
Sixth Day* Gen 1:31	Dies Veneris	Friga's Day	Friday	Viernes
Seventh Day** Gen 2:1-3	Dies Saturni	Saturn's Day	Saturday	Sabado

* In the New Testament the sixth day is also called the Preparation Day see Matt. 27:62; Mark 15:42; Luke 23:54

It is also observed as the "Preparation" day in the Old Testament. See Exodus 16:23-30. Notice the triple miracle every sixth day. Double fell on Friday, none fell on the Sabbath, Friday's portion never spoiled when kept until Sabbath.

**The Seventh Day is also called "Sabbath" (which means "rest") in both the Old and the New Testaments. See "Sabbath" in Lev. 23:31,32; Matt. 28:1; Mark 16:1,2; Luke 23:56 – Luke 24:1.

###In 150 countries in our world the Seventh Day is called "Sabbath," "Sabado," "Subota," "Shabat," etc. etc.

The ages when the world used the Latin and the Saxon names for the days of the week were times of great paganism and these names were derived from the pagan gods which the people worshipped at that time. It is interesting to see how those names were changed from the names which God gave the days of our week.

A Bit of the Rest of the Story

Bruce, my husband, and I were so happy to have a house of "our own." Of course, the bank owned most of it, but it was in our name, and we hoped that someday we would really "own" it. Each time we were transferred to a different city we tried to get just a bit larger and better house. We were investing in our future. In 1979 - 1980 we were living in Illinois, just north of Chicago when out of the blue we received a letter urgently asking us to become missionaries in Mexico. We considered it a real privilege and were happy to go. So, we packed up our things and listed our house and were on our way.

However, things in Illinois had suddenly taken a down-turn at that time and almost overnight houses were not selling well. We trusted God to take care of us since we were answering His call. We later discovered that there were 600 houses for sale just in our county alone. While our house was waiting to sell, it was vandalized: someone even took out the trees we had planted and broke the large mirrors in all the bathrooms. At this time our missionary salaries were not very large. Bruce's salary was $200 (yes, hundred) a month, and mine was $190 a month. He was paid in dollars, I was paid the equivalent in pesos.

We had accepted this call "for life" and truly expected to live there until Jesus came back or we died. With our small incomes and three children in Christian schools in the U.S.A (the youngest son was still living at home with us) there was no way we could pay our $1,000 per month house payment in Illinois. All of our investment and savings was in that house, but we were between a rock and a hard place. The bank offered to "take back" the house, but we would lose everything we had invested in it. We prayed and felt this was God's leading and if we ever would need to buy another house, He would provide it for us.

God's plans are just not always what we think they might be and in the mid 1980's we had to return to the U.S. Where would we go? What would we do? Someone suggested that Bruce write to several Christian colleges and let them know he was available to teach in the coming school year. There was a miscommunication and word went out that Bruce had already received a position teaching for the next year. By the time we learned about this, it was too late to obtain a teaching position for that fall so we had no job, no nothing. Oh! What to do?!?!?!?!?!?!??

Three of our children were going to school in Keene, Texas at that time so we chose to settle in that area. The girls' dean kindly let the two of us stay in a room in the girl's dorm for a week until school started and by then we were to find a house to put our home into. We had friends in Arlington, and it was a nice medium-sized town halfway between Dallas and Fort Worth so we figured that would be a good place to begin. It would give Bruce a better opportunity to find work in one of those two large cities.

Bruce got a newspaper and read the ads. He found one that said they had new houses for rent. We decided to check that out and found one that would be suitable for us, so he made an appointment to talk with the renter. It was a builder who had over-built, and he was very anxious to have us rent one of his houses. He knew that we had no job, no prospects (yet), no income, and 4 children in Christian schools, he was just glad to have his house rented! God took care of our housing needs.

Teaching jobs were all filled, Bruce had been out of scientific labs for several years and so people figured he was too "rusty" for them, or he was so over-qualified for the job available that he would leave the minute something he was qualified to do came available. Then a recruiter who was trying to help him find work, asked Bruce if he would be willing to work with them. They needed a scientific professional on their team, someone who could understand scientific things so that they could recruit scientists for medical and/or industrial businesses. Bruce is not a salesman; he had never done anything like recruiting people to place them into jobs, but we prayed and decided that if that is what God wanted us to do, He would bless Bruce's efforts so we would know that is where He wanted us to be. Bruce agreed to try it. God blessed Bruce more than we had ever dreamed possible. We were able to buy a new car for ourselves and even a new one for our oldest son.

Then one day we got a letter in the mail saying that the builder we were renting from had gone bankrupt and we had one of two choices. Buy the house at the price he was asking, a very inflated price and the house was not worth that amount, or we would have to get out at the end of the month. Again, we had to go house-hunting.

God certainly works in interesting ways! We thought we would go into an apartment until we had a bit more time to establish ourselves in that area. We paid a visit to an apartment locator to see what was available close to where we both worked. She had almost no apartments available. But she told us that she did have a house, a brand new one which the builder desperately wanted someone to live in. He had just had all of the installed carpets cut out of it and stollen. Therefore, he wanted it occupied ASAP.

So again, we moved into another brand-new house. We enjoyed it. Then six months later the whole bottom fell out of the job market. There were absolutely NO placements. Bruce's employer badly wanted him to stay because he needed a professional scientist on his team. For several months he gave an advance of salary to every recruiter who had had no placements. Bruce had done so fantastically the first several months that he badly wanted him to stay there because he knew Bruce would do great once things picked up again. After a while the employer said he could give no more advances in salary. Things went from bad to worse and then they got even worse for us.

We had to lose both cars, we were spending only $8.00 a month at the grocery store each week (this was in 1986). Then Bruce said we will have to spend less next week. God was really trying our faith! My work was not enough to pay rent and food to say nothing of water, electricity, and school bills. This was quite a trying time for us. We had to really trust God and learn to lean only on Him.

Just when we thought we could hang on no longer, we got the idea to start recruiting on our own. There would be no boss or middleman, everything earned would be ours and God's. My boss offered Bruce a rent-free office space. We worked hard and got financially back to ground zero again. Then one day we got the idea to work out of our house, this was not a common thing back then, and there would be no additional office rent to pay, neither would we have to sit and inhale second-hand smoke!

About two years later we got another letter in the mail saying this builder had gone bankrupt. The bank wanted to talk to us. They wanted us to buy the house we were living in. We told the banker that we had no money for a down payment, we were self-employed with no secure income, and we didn't even have money for closing costs. The banker told us that they had so many foreclosed houses in Tarrant County that they were very desirous of having us buy this house. Then he told us that they would allow us to live in the house rent free for three months while they completed all the liens and paperwork against the builder. Then he told us that they would use those three rent-free months as our down payment. He went on to say that they would use our rental security deposit as the closing costs. He also promised to work with us on the self-employment issue. He said if you go three months without being able to make a payment you call us, and we will work out something. We do not want you to go homeless and we do not want another foreclosed house on our accounts. Then he told us what our monthly house payment would be. It was less than we had been paying in rent!

We felt that this was God's way of giving us a house of our own. We signed the papers making it "ours" even though the bank owned more of it than we did.

We lived in that house for a little over eleven years then we moved to Arizona to help take care of my parents. During that time houses had gone up in value and when we listed it, it sold in one week and we had enough money to buy another house in Arizona.

God loves us! Good times and bad, He always takes care of us. He gave us a house to put our home into even though we had lost it all when we went to work for Him full time. Oh, how many ways he has blessed us!

We can never out-give the Lord! We give Him with a teaspoon, He gives us back by the shovelful. We give with a fork; He gives back by the pitchforkful.

We were able do to recruiting from our home for over 20 years. This allowed us to shut the door, walk out and to be gone for extended times on many mission trips.

In the early 1980's, while Bruce and I were living in Mexico, our children were in Christian boarding schools in the U.S. Bruce's salary was $200. dollars a month, and he was paid in dollars. My salary was the equivalent of $190. per month, but I was paid in pesos. Since our children were in the U.S., we decided to put his dollars into the bank in Mexico (it was allowed to have dollars in a Mexican bank at that time.) Since I was paid in pesos and that was the currency where we lived, we decided to live on my salary. This was very satisfactory, and we let the dollars slowly accumulate in the Mexican bank.

It was always nice to have a day free from classes, which was rare with our busy schedules. One day I realized I had no classes to teach and as we were getting dressed, I asked him, "do you have any classes to teach today?" He only had the first period class, 7:30 a.m. that day. We made a spur of the moment decision, which was not common for us to do, and decided we would take our dollars out of the Mexican bank, drive up to the border and put our dollars in the American bank so we could use it for our children's tuition. We had accumulated a little over $2,000 at that time.

We went to the bank and asked to withdraw all of our American money and were told we had to leave the equivalent of one month's salary in their bank, so we left two hundred dollars there and took the rest of the dollars to the U.S. We deposited the cash we had withdrawn in our American bank and decided to spend the rest of the day visiting our children who were in school in a small town several miles down the road from the town where our bank was located. It was fun to be with our children, but we had to leave in the afternoon so we would be home before dark as the roads we had to drive in Mexico were not too safe at night.

The next morning, we woke up and were preparing for our day. We had a small portable radio in our home and Bruce liked to listen to the news from an American station in the mornings as he got dressed. That morning as he was listening, he heard the news that during the night Mexico had nationalized all the banks and if anyone had any dollars in a Mexican bank the dollars now belonged to the Mexican government and could not be withdrawn until further notice, and no one knew when that would be or how much of those funds could be withdrawn.

What a shock that was to us. Here God certainly demonstrated that He was in control of our lives. We had not planned to withdraw our money the day before, with our limited income and children going to school in the U.S., every penny was important to us, and God knew that. A few months later we were told "you can have your American money; we will give you nineteen cents for each dollar." We decided we would leave the $38 (ex 200) dollars there and see what happened. When we left Mexico to return to the U.S. to live, we withdrew our money, and we were given seventy-nine cents on the dollar. Again, we had opportunity to be thankful that we could trust God and He was in charge of our lives.

In the 2000's after our four children were grown and living on their own, Bruce and I were asked to do some special mission work in some countries outside of the U.S.A. We had the privilege of going to several different countries around the world to share God's love and the story of redemption in all the countries we visited.

It was very interesting for us to see firsthand how the "pagan" religions (so called) all had very vengeful gods. Their gods were constantly watching very closely to see if the people disobeyed or transgressed any laws or taboos. If the gods saw any of these mistakes or transgressions, those gods were quick to "get you" in one way or another. Many people were afraid of their gods.

In several pagan countries we visited, the people were taught that the gods wanted them to do something bad to others before the others had a chance to do something bad to them. This is totally contrary to what the Bible and God teach us about the "golden rule," that we should treat others as we would wish to be treated! In other countries, if someone harmed you, you could give special offerings and have the gods curse the person whom you presumed had hurt you. It was quite a frightening way to live.

The experiences which I want to share with you, were our experiences in the various parts of the countries which we visited. Usually, we were able to stay in one of the larger towns of the country, while our meetings were in some of the smaller villages about an hour's drive from where we stayed. If someone visited New York City in the United States and then wrote a book about what America was like, they would have certain opinions. If another person visited a small town in Iowa and then wrote a book about what America is like, the two books would be quite different. I do not claim to have a comprehensive knowledge about all the countries we visited, I just want to share our personal experiences. Africa is a large continent, some of its countries are small, others quite large and have several different tribes so a person's experiences may vary from one place to another even though it is the same country.

As we visited these countries Bruce gave many talks on the great love of God. The God we worship is not a vengeful god just waiting to punish us. He is totally loving and wants us to serve Him out of love. He wants to help us, not hurt us. This was a totally new concept to the people and when the people there realized this was what God is really like they were so very happy that God could be trusted and loved and did not have to be feared. The result of knowing God is so loving and kind was that many people and wanted to worship Him instead of their pagan gods.

I always had a special program for the Children, but I also gave talks to the adults. I gave health talks because sanitation is almost nonexistent in many places. Water is often scarce and must be reused. In one country I was giving a talk on how to keep our drinking water safe, and I said if you have only one bucket of water and need to wash your hands, dip a tin cup into the water and then take your hands away from the bucket. Wash your hands and rinse them away from the clean water in the backet. The lady who was translating my talk, looked at me and incredulously asked, "WHY?"

In many, maybe I should say most of these countries, women are second class citizens. They must do much of the hard work while their husbands sit around and discuss happenings with the other men of the village. Often the wife must walk a couple steps behind her husband. Sometimes he even leans his hand on her shoulder as they walk. As we were driving out to our meeting site in one of these countries which we visited, we passed a group of women sitting on the ground beside the road. These women were selling small piles of charcoal (three – four pieces), a few potatoes, tomatoes, onions, or bananas, etc. The man who was translating for Bruce in that country told us as we went past, "the woman over there is my wife. She is earning our living.

Then he continued "bragging" about her and said she carries our water from the river, she washes (by hand of course) my clothes and irons them (with a heavy iron heated over a wood fire) and she dungs our house. Houses out in rural areas were usually made of dried mud and the people had to take fresh cow dung and plaster it over the walls and the floors of their houses because it made the walls withstand the weather and last longer. The dried dung also helped to protect their homes from bugs. Wow! He was proud that she was teaching their daughters to do the same things. What about any work he did?

In another country the man who translated for Bruce told us, "It is not proper to hold hands as a husband and wife. That signifies that she is a 'bad' woman because she is leading him around." However, it was perfectly normal and proper for a man to hold another man's hand! My sweet husband always held my hand! He was so kind and loving, it was natural for us to hold hands. We tried to remember to refrain from doing so, but it was such a natural thing for us to do that we just gave up and held hands anyway. After a couple weeks had passed this same man said to both of us, "You can hold hands, it is obvious that you both love each other very much." Another small victory for the love of God towards us.

After seeing how women were treated in so many places, we decided to give talks on how to have a happy home. Just the very basics, but it definitely opened the people's eyes. At the end of our series of meetings, Bruce asked all the married couples to come forward. Then he "performed" a little ceremony renewing their marriage vows. He had a man translating for him, and I had a woman translating for me. The men repeated what Bruce said and the women repeated what I said.

Before we did this little ceremony, we had asked our main translator if the people actually kissed each other at their marriage ceremonies (since women were treated in such a belittling manner). He answered in the affirmative, but we didn't tell him why we wanted to know. When the couples were at the front and after they had repeated their vows, Bruce said, "Men, you may now kiss your brides." There was much giggling, but they did it. Then we handed out a little certificate to them listing some suggestions for a happy marriage.

The next evening, our translator told us that he had reported to the leaders in that area what had happened at our meeting the night before. He said, "I told them you had asked the married people to kiss." The leaders were rather taken aback and said, "well, did the people do it, did they like it?" Our translator told the men, "Oh, yes!" Hopefully there were some happier homes in that area after we left.

I would like to share some miscellaneous facts about things we learned while visiting these other countries. Some things were interesting and some of them a bit frightening. The people were lovely, loving, and so kind and helpful to us but some of their customs were quite new to us.

While we were in the Philippines, the Muslims were having an uprising in our area, so we had to be very careful where we went (no place alone, always someone local with us!). If our driver drove into a parking lot security people had long poles which had mirrors on the end. These were moved around underneath of the car to make sure no bombs were wired under there. When we went into a store, security people patted us down to make sure no weapons or bombs were strapped to our bodies. A man would pat down my husband and a woman would pat me down. Then one of them would look into my purse.

There were different factions of the Muslims, some much worse than others and just before we arrived there the cohorts of one of the more radical and violent groups had bombed a hole in the jail and sixty-five of their "friends" had escaped so everything was on high alert. A Muslim leader of the kinder faction came to our orientation meeting. He told us that his group was glad we were there because he knew we would help his people and we were clean-living like his people were. He also told us that he would give his own life if any of us had our lives threatened. He also said, "you will all have spies from the rebel Muslims in your meetings, you won't know who they are, but you don't need to be afraid of them as we will also have our people there to spy on the rebels and if anyone causes you any problem, we will remove them."

It took us about an hour to go from our hotel to our meeting site and another hour back to the hotel. We went out during the day, but it was dark when it came time to go back to the hotel. As soon as we got into our car to go back to the hotel a pickup truck with six to eight well-armed soldiers sitting around the bed at the back of the pickup began to follow us. They followed us all the way to our hotel and stayed there watching until we got inside safely. One night we were stopped by some armed men who were standing at the side of the road. As soon as the car we were in stopped, the pickup behind us also stopped and the soldiers in the back stood up and said, "They're with us, they are okay." And we were allowed to pass safely.

Our venue was in a large gymnasium which held about 2,000 people. All across the front there was a cement platform about four and a half feet higher than the main floor. Bruce stood on this platform while he talked so that he could be well seen by everyone in the audience. One night about half ways through his talk someone shook my chair. I looked around and did not see anyone and then I noticed that the basketball hoops were swaying. I also noticed that the man translating for him stopped talking, got a strange look on his face, and stared at Bruce. Bruce was so busy talking and concentrating on what he was saying that he just kept talking so the translator picked up and carried on also. The only thing I thought of was, it's an earthquake and Bruce is way over there and I'm way over here, how will they ever find us both. Afterwards the translator asked, "Didn't you feel the earthquake?" It was about a category six. That was a new experience for us.

There we also learned about some interesting foods. On our way home from our meetings at night we often saw little stalls/booths along the side of the road. There was usually one bare light bulb hanging over the "counter" and often several people standing around. It looked like the people were eating something, so we asked our driver what that was. He explained that it was baloot (I have used the phonetic spelling because I never learned whether it was balut or baloot but it sounds like a double oo). When we asked what that was, he said it was fertilized duck eggs in all different stages of development, up to just before the ducklings hatched. Maybe that is why the people ate it in the dark, it was too unpleasant to look at if you ate it when there was light, and you could see what you were eating. The people ate everything except the shell! It was considered a treat or a delicacy for them. Somehow in my way of thinking, eating a whole unhatched baby duckling, feet, beak, bones, feathers and all does not sound like a delicacy or a treat.

Another interesting food was durian. This fruit is oblong and about the size of a small watermelon or a large honey dew. It is brownish in color and has triangular bumps all over the outside. The odor of it is very strong and it is quite obnoxious to some people. If a person is riding in a car and you pass by where durian is being sold at the side of the road you quickly roll up your windows, but the odor comes into the car anyway. We were told that it smells "like hell" but tastes like "heaven." When a person cuts into this fruit, it looks like a very mushy, soft poached egg. We were told that it is quite a luxury, and we MUST try it. We finally got brave and did. I hope there is nothing that tastes like that in heaven! Many foreigners cannot take the first bite of it. I found that it could be eaten, but I would not choose to do so. However, the worst part of it was tasting it again and again, and again for two days afterwards.

Another interesting fruit was the jack fruit. Some of the locals invited us to their home and while we there they served us jackfruit. We were sitting around the table when two men came in, one was carrying this huge fruit, it was the size of a large oblong watermelon, and it had a lumpy skin. The other man had a newspaper and a machete. They put the newspaper down, put the jackfruit on top of it and then whack! with the machete. When it was cut open the flesh was quite soft, white, and pulpy. Imbedded in this were yellow, oblong-shaped pieces, these were the fruit that a person eats. You remove the yellow part from the white fleshy part with your fingers, but first of all you have to thoroughly oil your fingers otherwise your fingers will stick together. Evidentially the white part is quite sticky. The yellow part is quite pleasant to eat. Inside of the yellow part is a seed, which we were told the people can cook and then eat, the seed is rather large and looks sort of like a large oblong lima bean.

There were a lot of other very interesting and delicious fruits there which we enjoyed very much. We were treated with a ride up into the mountains and visited a pineapple plantation, where the workers cut a fresh pineapple right off the plant and gave us slices to eat. It was totally delicious!

I think one of the most interesting sights we saw was a family of five all riding on one motorcycle. The father was driving and had one child sitting almost on the handlebars in front of him. The mother was sitting behind the father, holding a baby on her lap, and the other child was riding behind the mother and hanging on to the mother's waist!

The people were friendly and lovely, and so thoughtful. However, when it came time for us to leave, we had to go through eight (8) security checks at the airport and while we were waiting for our plane to board, we saw the pilot and co-pilot walk through the waiting area each carrying two very large suitcases. It seemed like they knew they would be gone a long time. We found out that we had left on the last day on which flights were leaving there for quite some time. Even though we thoroughly enjoyed being there it is always good to get home, and not to have the surprise being "stuck" somewhere for an indefinite period of time.

In the late 1940's to early 1950's my father (Lloyd) had been called to help spread the gospel in Cuba. It was a beautiful country, so modern and clean, and the people were very friendly and kind. We really loved living there. In the late 1950's Bruce, my husband-to-be, and his parents lived in Cuba His parents were some of the last Americans to be able to leave Cuba because Fidel Castro came into power and made it a communist nation.

In 2002 Bruce and I were privileged to go to Cuba and do missionary work and spread the story of God's love. We felt especially blessed because at that time Americans were not allowed to visit Cuba, however after a special invitation by Castro and special permission from the American State Department we, along with a few others, were allowed to go there. We certainly looked forward to revisiting that beautiful island.

However, it was quite a shock when we arrived. That beautiful island, so modern and clean was a very sad place. The island itself was still beautiful, the people still kind and loving but all the buildings were very run-down and deteriorated, and lacking paint. The people were so oppressed. Everyone lived under constant FEAR. Everyone was totally controlled and kept ignorant of what was really going on in the world. Communism controls by keeping people in fear and ignorance.

I hardly know where to start but will give a few examples. We were privileged to be able to walk to the houses in which we had lived when our parents were working there. The small house where my mother, Elsie, along with my father, my sister and I had lived in, now had three other families living in it. The house my husband's parents had lived in was a large, good-looking house "back then" but when we saw it in 2002 it was run down and looked like it had not been painted since back then.

Cuba had had some very beautiful architecture, now everything was decrepit, run down, and needing paint. There was one house in downtown Havana which had been a wealthy one-family dwelling it now had 15 families living in it (we counted the electric meters on the outside). We were so happy to have my sister and her husband with us on that trip and one evening the four of us went out to eat at a restaurant. The Cuban government had good facilities for tourists, but their own people could not use these facilities, more on that later. The grown man who was our waiter began to talk with us. Bruce and I were blessed that we both spoke fluent Spanish, so we learned things most tourists do not. This man asked us if we had children. We said yes but they were all grown and married. His next question was, "do they live with you?" When we said no, he wondered where they lived. He was surprised to learn that they all had their own houses and inquired how it was possible for them to do that. Are there enough houses available for them to live in by themselves, just their own family? Did they have to have permission from the government to move to their own houses? When you visit communist countries, you often learn more about the people and things by the type of questions people ask about your country and what they say when you are with them in private than by what you see or are told in public.

We were driven to most of our appointments in a 1942 Ford! The people had removed the trunk and added a seat in that area so two people could ride back there. We were with a friend, and this was in private so Bruce asked when a car broke down, and could no longer be fixed, did they take it to the "junk" yard. "Oh, my no, we don't have any junk yards, we take the car apart and use all the parts to fix other cars!" It was illegal for any common person to have a car newer than 1957, when a person died that person was not allowed will his car to a family member. The government told the family what was to happen to that car.

Our driver constantly looked in his rear-view mirror to see if we were being followed. One afternoon as he brought us back to our hotel he started to bang on the steering wheel in an excited manner and say, "Look! Look! Look!" When we asked what we were to look at, he pointed upwards to the top of our hotel and there we saw the American flag flying. He was thrilled to see that flag and told us the hotel had only put it there because the government told them to do so because we were staying there. The communists know how to put on a good front for the visitors. But it is very different for their citizens.

Our hotel was nice and clean, and we enjoyed a lovely breakfast buffet every morning. But no Cuban person could even enter the hotel, unless they worked there and if any visitor complained about any of the employees, that employee was immediately fired. Because Bruce and I both spoke Spanish well, we were not afraid to leave the hotel and walk around town a bit in the afternoons when we were not busy. When we would leave the hotel the people on the street would ask us if we had soap (meaning bath soap) in our hotel. Of course, we had the average small bars of hotel soap in our room so we answered in the affirmative, then they would ask if we had any left-over pieces and if so, could they please have them. We were told later that women would often stand outside of the hotel and offer to prostitute their young daughters (about twelve years old) if the tourist would give them these small bars of soap.

Even though we were fed a lovely breakfast, the Cubans went hungry. If a family had a banana tree or papaya tree in their back yard, it was closely watched and when the ripe fruit disappeared off of the tree, someone from the government would ask where the fruit was. If the person said they had shared it with a neighbor, the tree owner was punished for working against the government. If the owner said it had been sold, there was an even heavier punishment for working against the government. It was considered illegal to help a family have more food than that family was allowed to purchase with the coupons issued by the government each month.

Each family received a coupon booklet to buy groceries for the whole month. The coupons given were determined by the size and age of the members of that particular family. The amount allotted for an adult per month was not enough to feed a grown person for a week, any other food the person was able to obtain had to be grown (if there were space in your yard) or purchased on the black market but the costs there were prohibitively high for the common people. Therefore, almost all of the people had to do something "illegal" in order to have enough food to survive.

We would drive past a "grocery store" and notice that on the outside there was a hand-lettered sign with three or four items listed. That meant only those three or four items were available at that time. Also, there was always a guard at the door and usually a line of people waiting to get into the store. The shop owner could not allow more than two or three people into the store at once or he would have had chaos as everyone would push and shove and try to take one of the items he/she needed.

The pastor of the church which we were assigned to, was a 28-year-old man. He had a wife and two little boys. He rode in the car with us, but his wife could not come as there was not enough room for all of us in the car. On the way home from meeting one evening, we noticed a lovely-looking shop and several people lined up waiting to go in. We asked him what that was. He said, "it is an ice cream shop for tourists. Have you ever had ice cream?" We answered affirmatively and then asked if he had ever had ice cream and he told us that one time some was available so he and his wife, with his two little boys, walked to where it was being sold. The line went all the way around the block, and they had to stand in line for three hours. When it was their turn and they finally arrived at the ice cream place there was only one flavor left but they were glad to have the privilege of trying ice cream.

One evening he asked my brother-in-law if he had a car, using his American mind, he quickly answered, "yes, we have two" to which my sister just as quickly poked him in the ribs as if to tell him don't say anymore! Then our pastor happily told us that his father had had a Russian car but six years ago it had broken down and there were no parts available to repair it. On one of our journeyings we were able to do during the day, we drove past a vacant lot, and he pointed out a small blue car and told us it was his father's. He then told us that he, himself, was able to own a bicycle. He had had to ask the government for permission to get one and then when the permission finally came, he had to wait a long time until one was available for him to buy.

That was par for the way they lived. The government had to give permission to buy a fridge, the government told them they had to burn kerosene in their cooking stoves. The government had to give permission for them to travel from one town to another. Every aspect of their lives was controlled by the government.

Each block had a "captain" which means this person was a spy, he had to report to his superiors everything that went on in his block. This is how the government knew what you were doing with the fruit on your tree! Then his superior had to report to his superior and so on up the chain until the government had control of literally every aspect of and happenings in their lives.

One day we were invited to eat lunch at the home of one of the ladies who had been a playmate of mine when I was a child. Her mother did domestic work for the different missionary families. She went to a different home each day of the week, Sunday through Friday. The missionary salary was very low, and we could ill afford this luxury, but this dear lady had to support her children, so we hired her in order for her to help her family survive. When this lady came to work, she would bring her daughter with her, and I would play with the daughter, we had so much fun!

When we arrived at the apartment where my ex-playmate, now grown woman lived, we noticed that she had her own fridge. It was a small blue one. She told us it was 50 years old and if it broke down, she could not get permission nor did she have enough money to get another one, or to have it repaired. The dishes she served us on, had belonged to Bruce's mother and when Bruce's parents had to leave Cuba because Castro was in control, his mother had given the dishes to this lady. Can you imagine that in 2002 we were fed lunch on plates that Bruce's mother had given away some forty years earlier because she had to flee the country? I have no idea how this poor lady got enough food to feed us. Those are questions that you do not ask, you just graciously accept and certainly appreciate their hospitality.

The church we were assigned to, was an average-sized church, but it was packed every night, often even people standing in the aisles and in the back. We were told that we would have spies there every night and after the meeting, these spies had to go back and report everything that had happened that night to the "minister of religion" (the government) after the meeting each evening. Bruce would always stand at the back and shake hands as the people went out and he said he could tell who the spies were because they had such cold, dead, hard eyes. He had to be very careful what he said from the pulpit, or the government would have shut us down immediately. Religion and anything religious (even Christmas) had been banned for so long the people were hungry to hear. It seemed they could not hear enough about Jesus.

It seems that most people have a God-shaped hole in their hearts. When you invite God into your heart, you are happy. If everyone is commanded not to talk about God, Jesus, heaven, or the Holy Spirit, that God-shaped hole in their hearts has to be filled with something. The evil one has taken advantage of that empty hole and come in to fill that space with his ideas. There is a lot of Santeria, spiritualism, in Cuba.

We met a young woman whose husband was in the Cuban Navy. Therefore, he had to travel to other places in the world and he would sneak some "goodies" to her when he came home. Because of that she had some things that the common people did not have. Because her husband was gone quite a bit, she had to fill her time with something, and she turned to Spiritualism. She enjoyed communicating with the spirits and all the other things it provided to her. Someone noticed that she was interested in "spiritual" things and began talking to her about the Bible and the loving God of the Bible. Of course, this was taboo, but she began to enjoy hearing the loving things she was learning about God from the person who was teaching her.

The person who was talking to her about the Bible was a member of the church to which we were assigned. So, this young woman was invited to attend the meetings. She was happy to do so and planned to go. Our meetings were to begin on a Friday night. Friday afternoon her spirit counsellors came to her and told her in no uncertain terms, "If you go to those meetings, we will kill you." That frightened her quite a bit, but the friend who had been teaching her was so loving and kind this young lady made up her mind she would go on Friday night, just to see what it was all about. Our meetings always began on a Friday night, we had another one on the morning of the seventh day, another one that evening, and every night Sunday through Friday. It was not frightening but comforting happy and loving.

This young lady came on Friday night, and she felt such peace and enjoyed what she heard, and she decided to come back the next morning. She did come on the morning of the seventh day, however, before the meeting had ended, she suddenly got the worst headache she had ever had in her life. She knew the spirits would carry out their promise to kill her and were doing just that. Therefore, she decided that maybe she should not go back that evening. What she did not know was that beginning on Friday night and each time there was a meeting a small group of people would gather in a little room at the back of the church and pray specifically for her. They prayed for the meetings as a whole but knew her life had been threatened so they prayed especially for her.

At noon she went home and sometime during the afternoon her headache disappeared. When it did not come back, she decided to go through with her plans to attend the meeting that evening. The headache never came back, and she faithfully attended every meeting. At the end of the series of meetings, there was a baptism, and she was one of those who chose to be baptized. As she came up out of the water, she had the most beautiful smile on her face and such a look of pure peace on her face. She was truly happy.

But her husband was not a happy person, he was so angry that he decided to leave her, and he took all of the things he had given her with him. My sister was about the size of this young lady and so gave her a couple of dresses. This young lady was able to continue coming to the meetings and learning that God is love and does not threaten, but helps, those who are trying to obey Him.

There is a wonderful and interesting thing about God. If a person needs to "give up" something in order to follow and obey God. God always gives them something much better!

The church to which we were we were assigned, was situated in the large city of Havana, however, there was only one hymnal in the whole church and that was reserved for the pianist. The people are happy to learn all the songs by heart. They learned quickly and they certainly sang the songs with their whole hearts. It was beautiful. The people are very sincere, and church is special to them. They wear their best clothes and are always as clean as possible.

Whenever a man goes on the platform, he is expected to wear a suit coat, even in the heaviest heat, to show respect and reverence to God. People cannot afford to buy a suit or even a suit coat, so the church has solved that problem by having one suit coat in the pastor's office and whenever a man goes onto the platform, he wears that coat. People are not all the same size, so you see some interesting things. The song leader would come onto the platform wearing a coat, when he walked off the platform, another man came out to make announcements, he was wearing the same coat. When that man walked off the platform another man would come out to offer a prayer and he was wearing the same coat. Some people fit into the coat okay, others swam in it and for others the sleeves and coat were way too short. But they are doing their best to honor and respect God.

The reason that the church had so much as one hymnal is that a visitor from Canada had noticed the absence of hymnals and had sent a large box of hymnals so that each church in Cuba could have one hymnal.

One evening my sister and I needed to use the restroom. It was upstairs at the back of the church. One of the men (he was a deacon) asked whether we were going upstairs to the restroom. When we said, "yes." He told us to wait a moment and he would go with us and put the fuse into the box so that we could turn on the light. He said it was so hard to get fuses that they had to remove the fuse every time someone came out of the restroom, or the fuse would be stolen.

We had heard about how short the supply of soap was, so my sister and I decided that we would teach the people how to make soap. We knew that one of the things a person needs when making soap, is a good supply of grease to help make the soap. One day I was able to talk on the phone with the president of the conference where we were going, and I asked him could he please help us find a supply of grease. He answered me very carefully and said, "it is not available." So, I asked when someone butchers an animal isn't there grease? Again, he said, "it is not available." Now I understood he could not say more, and I dropped the question. After having lived in Cuba, I knew that the people often butchered their own animals, therefore, I thought this was a good question. After arriving in Cuba, I was told when you butcher an animal you have to report to the government what you do with every single part of that animal, even the nose, the tail, ear, the insides, everything. The man would have been accused of working against the government if he told them, "We gave it to the Americans so they could teach the people how to make soap." That was the way they had to live.

When we found out we could not teach the people how to make their own soap, we thought at least could bring little bit of bath soap to give to the church members. My sister and I began collecting things. Hand soap, toothpaste, toothbrushes, ball point pens, small things that we could give away, and a few pieces of fabric so they could make some items of clothing. Some things we bought, but being a nurse, she had some friends who were dentists, so she went to them asking for toothbrushes. Many dentists order them in quantity to give to their patients after a visit. Sometimes there is a mistake in printing of the dentist's name or address on the give-away brushes so they cannot use them. These were all donated to us.

We had about 400 toothbrushes to give away. After the meeting one night, we gave these out to the people as they left to go home. We had all types of brushes, regular brushes, brushes for false teeth, and children's brushes. The night we were giving out toothbrushes we ran out of them and only had children's brushes left so we gave them out. A sixteen-year-old girl on her way out, received a small children's brush. She immediately burst into tears, and she said, "thank you so very much. I have never had a toothbrush before, this one is all mine."

There is "free" medical service available to the citizens of Cuba. Even operations are free. However, there is a small problem. You can have any medical care which you need for free, but how would you like to have your operation with no anesthetic or other drugs? If you want anesthetic or any other drug, you must pay for it yourself. Of course, most people cannot afford this luxury.

One of the most beautiful beaches I have ever seen is located about forty miles east of Havana. When I was a child, we used to love going there for the day. Everyone enjoyed that beach. When we were there in 2002, we wondered if it would be possible for us to visit it again. A friend agreed to take us one day. We were so thankful to him for taking us. But he couldn't tell us thank you enough times for letting him take us. He explained that the government had shut down all the beaches except for government employees but because he was the driver for tourists, he was allowed to enter the beach. Their beaches are beautiful, and the Cuban people loved their beaches but could not use them. By his taking us there it at least gave him a chance to see it, he might never have that opportunity again. There were tourists from Canada and several other European countries there, but we were the only Americans.

Even though that beach is only forty miles from Havana, we were stopped by military men with guns five times in that short ride. Who is in the car? Where are you going? Why are you going? We were stopped coming and going. No one trusts anyone else. Who is spying on you now, who is going to give a false report just because they may not like the way you happened to look at them sometime.

Those poor people! There is so much more I could say, I could write a book! But this gives you a little idea of what it is like in a communist country. I have been told that in the twenty plus years since we were there in 2002, it has gotten much worse. Cuba is a beautiful island, the people are so lovely, there are so many natural resources that could benefit people, but they can't be used or enjoyed by the average citizen, only tourists or higher-up government employees.

You may wonder how the people can survive in that atmosphere. They do it with humor. The have many jokes which are told in private. They shared some of these with us and I will share one with you, but first I must give you a bit of information.

In some countries where there are many bugs, a bug-killing liquid called "flit," is available to the people in these countries, you put the liquid into a tube with a pump at the end. It sort of looks like a bicycle tire pump with a small container on the end. You pull the handle back and then push it forwards and the spray comes out and hopefully kills the bugs. In English this is call a "flit gun." In Spanish they call it a "flit bomb" but because the grammar in Spanish has the words flipped to make it grammatically correct, in Spanish it is called a "bomba de flit."

A man had some bugs he needed to kill so he bought a flit gun and he put it into a paper bag to carry it home. As he was walking down the street, he met a military policeman. The policeman stopped him and asked, "what is in the bag?" The man was very frightened and didn't say anything, so the policeman asked him again, "what is in the bag?" Finally, the man decided he better do something, so he just shook his head "no." The policeman kept asking and the man kept shaking his head. By now the policeman was quite angry so he grabbed the paper bag from the man's hand, opened it, and looked inside. When he saw the harmless flit gun he told the man, "Why didn't you just say it was a 'bomba de flit?" The man was still afraid, but he said, "If I told you, it was a 'bomba de flit' you would have shot and killed me right after I said 'bomba' and I would not have been able to finish saying that it was just a 'bomba' de flit in the bag!"

It is sad but true that total control or total power leads to great corruption and many evils.

Another place Bruce and I were happy to serve was the continent of Africa. We were there three times, a different country each time. The countries were all very different from each other. We were in Nigeria, Kenya, and Ghana.

We went to Nigeria in 2003, it was the first African country we were in. It is a truly beautiful country. The people were lovely, but the country itself is quite corrupt. They have oil, but who knows what happens to it as the people are extremely poor. It is the only country we have been in where the people are the "beasts of burden." Instead of a horse or ox pulling a cart, it would be a man. The women also carried very heavy loads on their heads and even small children had to help carry loads.

We stayed in one of the larger cities, but our venue was in an area about an hour from our hotel and this area was surrounded by many smaller villages. We had our meetings outside in the evening.

We noticed some very interesting things in this city. As we were being driven to the different places, we would see signs printed on walls or buildings, "do not urinate here." Often, we would see men doing that very thing right beside the sign. Some other interesting signs we saw in the city said, "this building is not for sale. When we asked why anyone would put up such a sign, we were told that unscrupulous businesspeople or "realtors" would sell a house receive the down payment, or more, for that house. Give the buyers their "papers of ownership" and arrange with the new owners for their move-in date. When the day to move in arrived, and the new owners came to their house to move in, the "old" owner was still living there and said we have never sold our home. The new "owner" would then try to go to the businessperson or realtor who had sold the house to them, but no such person existed or could not be found. The buyer was just out of his money, and it was his tough luck!

Corruption was rampant from the government down to the ordinary citizens. What happened to all the money from their oil wells? Schools were minimum, roads were in terrible disrepair, it was just everyone for himself. Garbage was everywhere! When someone had something to throw away, they just dropped it wherever they were. There were huge piles of garbage, not just trash, but stinky garbage along the side of the road, and often it spilled across a good half of the road. Our driver would just go around it and go on our way. I suppose sometime, someone picked up a part of it.

The gentleman who drove us back and forth told us a local man had gone to the United States, taken medicine and was a successful doctor in America. His brother had a position of power in the government in Nigeria and wrote to his doctor brother and asked for some help fixing the poor roads. The doctor sent a very sizeable check to help his people "back home" but the money and the brother just disappeared. The roads stayed in the same disrepair.

When we drove around the city the driver would try to go around the huge potholes in the road. One night it had rained quite heavily so the road was covered with water and the driver did not see the pothole, so he accidentally drove into it, and we were stuck. The water came in under the doors and our feet were swimming in it. All I could think of was "do not urinate here" and wondered what else was in that water! The driver and the man riding with us got out of the car and called for some large guys standing idly on the sidewalk beside the road and all of them just lifted the car (it was a rather small car) with Bruce and me in it out of the pothole and we went on our way. You adapt and enjoy it.

The hotel we stayed in was rather unique. There was a sign in the bathroom saying, "do not use the toilet paper unless nature deems it necessary, and do NOT take it home with you." That was a new one for us! We would not have wanted to take it home with us, but at least we did have "toilet paper," and a real toilet.

As usual, there were a small group of us who were there as visiting missionaries. Each person arrived separately but we all stayed at the same hotel and were driven out to our different venues each evening. One of the men in our group was quite persnickety. He brought two white towels with him and put one down on the little desk in his room, then he carefully arranged some food stuffs on it which he had brought from home. These he covered up with the other white towel. One of the things he brought was a box of cookies. When he opened his cookies, he parceled them out carefully so he would have enough to last until he went home. Finally, he finished the whole top layer of cookies and lifted off the divider between the two layers, the whole bottom layer was gone. It seems that the men who cleaned the rooms had enjoyed his cookies! He tried to cover things so carefully so no one would touch his food, and yet they had eaten the whole bottom layer of his cookies!

Another man who was in our group came back to his room after his meeting one night. He always double locked his room before he left it, but this night when he came back there was only one lock which was locked. He thought it odd but was so tired he just put on his pajamas and went to bed; he did not hang up the clothes which he had taken off. He had not been in bed long when he thought he heard a sound coming from the closet where his clothes were kept. He stayed still and listened carefully. When he heard the sound again, he grabbed the flashlight which he kept beside his bed and quickly turned it on and shined it towards the closet. Imagine his surprise when he saw two white eyeballs staring back at him. He got up and turned on the room light and noticed that his pants had also grown legs! When people are so black, the whites of their eyes and their teeth really shine out in the dark! He hollered at the man behind his clothes in the closet and the man quickly fled the room.

After looking into the matter the next day, he found out the man in his closet had been one of the men who cleaned the rooms and the "security" guard had let him into the guest's room that night hoping the man could find something he could use for himself and share with the "security" guard as payment for opening the room for him. Our friend had come home from the meeting sooner than the intruder expected. We thought security guards were meant to protect.

One of the couples in our group had $50 (American) taken from their room on another night. The people in those countries are so poor that whatever little we have makes it seem like we are rich and so these people feel they have a right to share the wealth.

Another interesting sign which we saw was posted outside of an "eatery." It could have been a small café or just a small stand beside the road, but there would be a sign saying, "food is ready." That meant the establishment was open for business and there was food! We sort of thought if it was an eatery there would be food there. Soon we began to see signs saying "104" is ready. That got our curiosity and when we asked about that we were told that "104" meant dog.

As we rode around the rural areas, we would see people standing beside the road holding up skinned carcasses of whole animals. When we inquired about these we were told, "it is bush meat, the people think bush meat is much better than domestic meat." Bush meat could be anything from monkeys, opossums, armadillos, huge rats, cat, dog, wild pig, or any animal caught in the wild.

Usually, the pastor drove us in his car, but there was also another man who would sometimes drive us in his car, as there were two cars at our venue. Whoever was our driver would usually pick us up by himself but after the meeting when it was dark another man always rode with us. The two men in the front, Bruce and I in the back. We had some most interesting conversations with them. The second driver was quite a large man, and he was often the one who was the extra rider when the pastor drove us. He told us that his father was a medical doctor and during the 2nd world war he had gone to Russia to work for the Russians. While there he met and married a Russian lady, and they had two children. After the war he brought her and their two children back to Nigeria to live in his hometown, which was where we had our venue. Soon all the neighbors wanted to eat her, because they thought white meat would taste better than black meat. This frightened her so much that he had to move her into the town where our hotel was, but the neighbors there wanted to eat her also. She was so frightened that she packed herself and two children up and went back to Russia. Then the father married a black lady, and this man who rode with us and was also our second driver at times, was one of their sons.

He asked if we remembered the Biafran war of 1977 - 1979. We said yes, so then he said we all liked it very much because we got to eat all of the enemy soldiers who we killed during that war. We had lots of fresh meat at that time. He told us that the people living there had been cannibals until quite recently. Then he added, "but don't worry, we won't eat you!" To be honest, until we heard that we had not even thought of the fact that we might be eaten in our day and age!

We soon discovered why an extra person always rode along with us back to our hotel every night. There was quite a bit of unrest in that area and our people wanted us to be safe. Our driver did not always take the same road back to the city, that was also a safety precaution. One night on our way home, the pastor who was our driver that night, suddenly stopped, turned off the motor and the car lights. Both he and the extra rider put their windows down and each one put his head out the window on his side of the car. The two men quietly listened for a little while, talked to each other in their language, and then turned on the car and went a little farther. Then the whole process was repeated again. At the third stop I asked, "would you like me to say a prayer for us?" "Oh yes, please do." So, I did, and then we continued on to the hotel with no more episodes.

A few nights later, two men on motorcycles followed behind our car even though we had the driver and our rider with us. Bruce and I really didn't pay much attention to it until our driver suddenly turned off the road onto what turned out to be no more than a trail between grasses that were higher than the car on both sides of the trail. The path wound around and around, and we could not see very far ahead of us. The driver explained that this was a private path, a shortcut to another road and would be safer for us to take than the regular road. He said, "I know the gate man at the other end. He sleeps in a little building right beside the gate and when we get there, I'll wake him up and he can open the gate and let us out and we'll be on a good road again." We eventually got to the little guard house by the gate and the driver got out to waken the guard, but he wasn't there that night! We were stuck and could not get out to the good road. The driver was very disappointed but there was nothing to do except turn around and go back to the road we had been on before.

Somewhere about where we had suddenly turned off the road onto the trail, we had lost our two motorcycle friends, but neither Bruce nor I noticed. It was a small car and sitting in the back we did not see everything as well as the two men in the front. We got into town safely and were almost at the hotel when two motorcycles approached us. The driver stopped and so did they, it was the two men who had followed us when we left the meeting site obviously our driver had recognized them. They told our driver that somehow, they had lost us and were so worried something bad had happened to us that they rode all the way to the hotel to see if we were there and discovered that we had not arrived there, their only option had been to turn around and now were on their way back home.

We learned a lot of interesting things from our drivers as we were on our way out to the meeting site every afternoon. I guess the ride back to the hotel in the dark was a bit stressful and the driver had to pay closer attention to what was happening as he drove along, so we didn't talk so much at night. We often saw a hose sticking out of the top at the center off a palm tree. When we asked about that we were told they were making palm wine. It is easy to do, cheaper for the people who buy it, and it gives income to the person harvesting it. The only problem is that once that has been done to a palm tree it dies.

These people are so poor that they live on what they can gather, and they don't think too much about what will happen in the future when they destroy things in nature. One day we saw a beautiful bird, we really hadn't seen too many birds even though there were a lot of trees. Our driver told us the name of the bird, and said that the people really enjoyed eating that bird's eggs. The boys would climb the tree, rob the eggs from the nest and then they'd have a good meal. I asked him how they were going to have new birds to lay more eggs if the boys took all the eggs out of the nest. That was a totally new idea to him, and he had never thought that something like that could happen. The boys had found food for that day and that was enough for their family.

With all of the trees, tall grass and bushes in that area we asked if there were any snakes in their area. We got an interesting answer, "oh, no we have no snakes here, only serpents."

I mentioned the potholes in the roads in town. Out of town it was worse. The potholes got so large it was not possible to drive on the road, so people just drove off the road on the grass and then back up on to the road. After a while even the "detour" around the pothole got potholes so sometimes the people who lived close by would put a few shovels full of dirt into the pothole to smooth it out a bit. Then these men would take a long stick and hold it across the road so you could not pass. These people expected you to stop (you had no choice!) and give them a few pennies. This is the way some people earned a little money to buy a few daily necessities. Again, one day at a time, just enough for today.

One of the things we found most interesting was that the seventh day of the week in the Nigerian language is called "the Lord's Day," or "God's Day." However, the first day of the week, Sunday to us, is called "obuasi day" which means the white man's day. Our driver explained to us that this was because the Nigerian people had always worshipped God on the seventh day. How did this get started? Remember the Ethiopian Eunuch who went to Jerusalem to worship God and the Queen of Sheba who went to visit King David? Both of these important people were from Africa and I'm sure they took the knowledge of the true God which they had learned from the Israelites back to Africa with them and taught their people about God.

So why did Sunday become known as "the white man's day"? Because when the white man, Spanish priests, came to Africa they told the Nigerians they were worshipping on the "wrong" day of the week and told them they had to worship on Sunday! When the Nigerians found out that it was not God (who has told us in the Bible that He never changes) who changed the day of worship from the seventh day to Sunday but that it was a change in God's commandments made by a mere man who claims to be god on earth, this information made them very glad to know they had been worshipping God on His day as He had told people to worship Him. We found this to be true in other African countries also.

Before Bruce gave his talk, I always had a program for the children. There were always a lot of children and they really enjoyed something special which was just for them. Usually, the children just had to sit and listen to the adults while their little feet dangled in the air, or they sat on the ground. An adult with a long stick used to walk along the rows of children and if anyone was caught talking or giggling, they were hit on the head with a stick! When the children were given something just for them and it was so interesting, they did not need to be hit on the head in order for them to sit still and listen.

Our meetings were held outdoors and when we first visited the site, there was a lot of trash thrown everywhere. There were several children standing around watching everything and I asked them to please help make it clean and pretty for the meetings. They were so glad to help and went to work immediately, picking up every piece of trash. It looked so nice, and then I realized that they were just taking the trash to the edge of the woods and dumping it all right there! After all, the adults just dumped stuff wherever they felt like it and the ground where the people would be sitting was cleaned up.

I mentioned the large piles of garbage all over the roads. When we visited in the homes of the people, I saw why. If a person in the house had garbage, it was quickly disposed of by dropping it out of the closest window, or right outside the back door. This gave me added "fuel" for my health talks. I did not say "don't" throw your garbage out by the back door, but I did tell them when they had trash, it should be taken away from the house and burned. If there were garbage to be disposed of, a pit should be dug away from the house and the garbage dumped in the pit. If possible, it should be covered. Then I said when garbage is too near our homes it brings rodents and bugs and these cause diseases to us and our children. When people have not been taught principles of hygiene the simplest things have to be explained in detail and a reason given so the people will see the necessity of doing things differently.

I have said that our venue was about an hour from the hotel where we were staying, so in order to get to the venue, set everything up for the evening meeting, and take everything down afterwards and then drive another hour back to the hotel we had to leave about three or three thirty in the afternoon and we did not get back until about nine that evening. That is quite a long while to be gone. Especially in some of these third world countries where you are not sure what types of not-so-interesting "bugs" you can pick up from the food you eat.

One tries to be very careful, but there is always the possibility something can happen. Because of that fact, I always tried to find out what restroom facilities were available for our use. In Nigeria, a lot of the people understand English, so when we were visiting the venue for the first time, I asked one of the ladies standing there, "where is the restroom?" I knew she understood English because I had been talking with her in English. When she did not answer, I thought she had not heard me. Therefore, I asked again. After the third time I asked, she just pointed to a "building" off to the back. I figured since I had asked, I'd better go and at least act like I used the facilities. When I went back there, I discovered what the "facilities" were. It was four and a half walls, no roof, and no floor except the dirt of the ground. I say half wall, because the fourth wall had an opening which served as a door, but there was no door. That is all! You did your business right onto the ground. If it was urine it soaked into the dirt. If it was solids, you did not need to worry about it because the chickens would come and eat it up. If the chickens did not eat it, the pigs certainly would. If not their animals, then the neighboring animals would.

Another night on the way home, the driver took yet another road back to the hotel. We were thankful that he knew where he was going because we certainly did not recognize anything. We were slowly driving along in the dark, with the condition of the roads, you definitely did not drive fast, especially in the dark. Plus, the driver had to keep an eye out for anything out of the ordinary.

This night down the road a little way from us, we could see something in the middle of the road. As we got closer, we could see it was a large white plastic "bucket," the type of five-gallon plastic buckets which painters use. At the bottom of it, was a burning candle. We could see no one anywhere nearby. There was a house to the left, but it was set quite a way back from the road. Then up ahead, on the road about a quarter of a mile from where we were, we could see another large white plastic bucket with a candle burning in it. Obviously, someone had set up a private roadblock to stop anyone driving past, and probably there were no good intentions in mind after the vehicle had been stopped. Our driver was extremely cautious as he began to drive past. He went even slower than normal. If someone were hiding in the bushes, and you did not stop, you would probably have been shot. When we were well past the last bucket our driver continued on as normal.

We always asked God for His protection when we got in the car to go somewhere, and we certainly felt His protection in Nigeria.

On another evening we were on our way back to the hotel on still a different road than we had used previously. Everything was going fine; the driver and our extra rider were in the front and Bruce and I in the back. The driver began going slower and slower and the two men in front began talking to each other in Nigerian. Then we were asked to roll up our windows. I was sitting behind the passenger seat and stretched my head to see out the front. I could see a very large log placed across the roadway. When we came to the log our driver had to stop. When we stopped, I could see four or five good-sized men standing on the bank of the road at the passenger side, the side where I was sitting. The rider in our car jumped out and began vigorously talking to the men standing there. After a little while he got back in the car and talked seriously with our driver. All the conversations were done in Nigerian, it was obvious they did not want us to know what was being said as both of them regularly talked English with us. When their conversation was over, the driver jumped out and began seriously and strongly talking with the men at the side of the road.

There was some type of argument going on. Bruce and I were sitting in the back quietly praying. I kept thinking if they get us, they'll take all our money then what will we do? I had made small cloth "money belts" for each of us and we always wore these inside of our underwear, under our clothes. We would never leave any cash in our room. These little money belts were totally unobtrusive and by planning ahead, we could take out just a small amount of cash for necessities before we left our room. I did not think if they "got us," we probably would not have been left to worry about money!

After quite a bit of arguing back and forth the driver again came back and got into the car and a couple of the men at the side of the road, walked out and pulled the big log out of the road so we could go by. As we drove past, I looked out the window to my right and saw that one of those men was holding a very large club, like a baseball bat, in his hand. He had it hidden from sight but in driving past I very clearly saw it. They certainly had no good planned for us but again God had His hands over us.

When we asked our driver and his companion who those men were, we were told "oh, they were vigilantes standing there to keep the road safe." Well, I never heard about vigilantes keeping the road safe!

These were some of the experiences we had when we were in Nigeria twenty years ago. I have heard recently that Christians there are now being persecuted much more. Satan does not like to give up his captives, but God's angels are much stronger and find ways to help those who are trying to obey God.

Then in 2005 we were invited to go to Kenya. We found things quite different there than they had been in Nigeria. There has been a much greater European influence in Kenya, people had more "things," used beasts for hauling carts, seemed to have copied more of the white man's culture and ideas. Again, our hotel was in a larger city about an hour's drive from our venue.

Our venue was in a smaller city, we were outside, right beside the main highway leading to the Congo (home of Idi Amin). The people had placed large loudspeakers facing out towards the main city market. They were not bashful to have everyone possible hear what was happening. Our platform was on a small rise, the hill went down in front of us, and up even higher to our right. The highway was to our left. Again, we were the only white people there. We did not count but were told that there were several thousand people there every night and, on the weekends, we were told it was ten thousand. We sort of felt like two grains of rice in a big pot of black beans. But everyone was kind and helpful to us.

I always made puppets for the children, using fabric as close to the skin color of the people in whatever country we were at. Of course, in the African countries my puppets were black-skinned. I had written skits for the puppets which coordinated with Bruce's sermon topic for each night. The skits were written as children talking and I had them translated into the appropriate language of the country which we were in. I had also written them in Spanish for the Spanish-speaking countries we visited. I asked four of the older local teenagers to manage the puppets for me. I had a large piece of heavy fabric which I hung up, the teenagers would stand behind the "screen," put the puppets on their hands and be able to move the puppets according to what the script said as they read it out loud to the children. The puppets were very inter-active with the children, often talking to the children and asking questions which the children could answer. The children always loved their "puppet show."

Each night I had a small giveaway I had made for the children, simple things like a felt hearts, felt butterflies, a 3x5 card with a picture of Jesus, another card with a worm and butterfly on it and the words printed, "Jesus changes me." These were just something small the child could take home to remind them that Jesus loved them. In many countries, it seemed like children were second class people and I wanted them to know that each child is important to Jesus. When we arrived in Kenya and we told the people that I had a children's program we were told, we cannot teach the children about the Bible until they are twelve years old, they would not understand. I told them that I had a program for the children and would use it every night.

We had so many people at our venue in Kenya because the people at our venue had invited several other smaller villages to come to this meeting site. We were told that over the weekends some of the people had walked all day to be there for the Friday evening meeting, these people would just sleep outside on the ground Friday night so they could be there for the meetings on the next day and Sunday. I do know that I had made 300 small giveaways for the children, and I ran out of them every night.

After a few days, the same person who had told us you cannot teach the Bible to children under twelve years old, told us, "It seems like the children under twelve really do enjoy hearing about the Bible stories." We were also told that beginning about two thirty or three every afternoon they could see children walking down the road, tugging on their parents' hands to hurry and get to the meeting site! We always found a large group of children sitting there quietly waiting for us to arrive, and shortly after we arrived and began setting things up you could see more children coming running over the hill so they could be sure to and get a place to sit on the ground. Everyone wanted to get as close as possible so they could see everything. Someone had put up a small cord all around the platform about five feet away from where we stood. They had done this to protect us from being squashed by the crowd. It looked very flimsy, but the people respected it.

One evening I talked about heaven and how tame all the animals would be. I asked if the children would like to pet a lion in heaven. "OH, NO!!!" I was surprised so I tried to explain that the animals there would all be tame and would not hurt anyone. But they still said a vehement no. The man who was translating for me told me, "I will pretend to be a lion and they can pet my head." So, in Swahili he said I am the lion, and he stooped over and walked in front of some of the children, but they shrunk away from him and totally refused to touch him, even though they knew he was just pretending to be a lion. These children knew how dangerous some of these wild animals could be and had great respect for the wild animals.

We saw baboons walking along side of the highway just as though we were the intruders and the highway belonged to them. We sometimes had to wait for the zebras to cross the road in front of us. One of the other couples who was in our group in Kenya had to wait while a black jaguar crossed the road in front of them one night while they were on the way to their venue. We did not see lions, cheetahs, elephants, giraffes, or other large game until we visited the Masai Mara after our meetings closed. When we checked in, we were told be sure to close your windows and door thoroughly because the monkeys like to get into the rooms and help themselves to anything that catches their fancy!

When we were holding our meetings, I always wore a flared black skirt, black knee-highs, and black shoes because it went with any colored top, and I never knew what or where I would have to climb up or on, and where we would end up going and I needed to be prepared for any situation. It was a modest and practical way to dress.

The man who was our interpreter wanted to show us some of the churches that were part of the group who came to our venue in Kenya, and we took time to visit some of these churches. Many were very simple and humble one-room buildings. Usually thatched roofs, dung walls, some had cement floors, all had plank "benches" with no backs. At one they had a nice large pile of bricks which the people were making so that they could have brick walls which are more durable than mud and dung walls.

One afternoon we were taken to a lovely small church which actually had brick walls and a tin roof. A group of about ten people gathered to greet us and we were standing around outside and talking after we had seen their building. One of the ladies there had her little girl, about two years old, with her. The little girl was quite shy and hid behind her mother's skirt but as children do, curiosity got the better of her and she soon came out of hiding and began to run around the group a little bit. I love children and so when she came close to me, I bent down to talk to her.

What a mistake! She took one look at me and just shrieked a terrified scream and ran away. It seems like she had seen my black clothes and what she thought were black legs because of the black knee-highs I was wearing, but when I bent down, she saw my face. I don't think she had ever seen such a strange, weird-looking white face in all her little life. She ran away to the far side of the church, and nothing could coax her to come back. When I bent down, she saw my white face and it was so different from anything she was used to that it gave her a terrible scare. I felt so badly to have frightened her and could not apologize enough but the adults from that area all had a good laugh.

As we were leaving the country of Kenya, we were taken to visit an old fortress by the sea. It had been used as a place in which to keep the captured Africans who were to be sold as slaves. Here we learned some interesting things. Many times, one African tribe would capture people from another tribe and would bring and sell their captives to the white man to be taken to other countries and sold as slaves. Another interesting fact we were told was that the British took and bought many more slaves than America had. We had always heard about slave trade in America, so it was a bit of a surprise to us to hear that the British took and used more slaves than America ever had.

Kenya having been a British colony for so long, they drive on the "wrong" side of the road. It took a bit of getting used to in order to ride on the left and have on-coming traffic to your right. We arrived late at night, obviously it was dark and several of us were riding in the same van on our way to the hotel. The driver was driving from the right side of the van, he had a passenger with him, and the passenger sat on the left (passenger side over there). The ride-along passenger was a friendly person and was trying to tell us about his country and make us feel welcome there. One of the ladies in our group had not been paying a lot of attention to what was going on and after we had been on the road awhile, she looked at me and said very quietly, "I do wish the driver would not keep turning around and being so friendly to us I wish he'd pay more attention to where he is driving!" Then I told her, "Edie, in this country they drive from the right side of the car, that man on the left is just a passenger." Then she could sit back and enjoy the conversation and the drive.

Kenya was the country where we were told that married people who were nice did not hold hands. That is also where Bruce had the married couples renew their wedding vows.

It was always interesting to go to a new country. We were also invited to go to Ghana in 2006. We tend to think of Africa as a large place, but it has many countries and each one is different than the others. We were in the center of the continent, both on the east side and the west side, and in the center itself. The central part of Africa is not as "westernized" as the southern part of Africa. But the different countries are interesting, and the people were always so friendly, kind, helpful, and very nice.

Ghana was the third country of Africa in which we held meetings. This was also a beautiful country with lovely people. Here our venue was much closer to the hotel where we stayed. We had only about a fifteen-minute ride to get there, and it was mostly in the city. Our venue here was outside again, but this time it was on the main square in the center of town. The square was surrounded by small stores, businesses and homes. The pastors had prepared a large, raised platform for us to stand on as we presented our talks. This made it easy for all the people to see and hear us well. The people also installed large loudspeakers facing outwards. This made it possible for many people to hear the whole program without ever leaving their homes or businesses. The square was full of people, judging by the size of our groups at other venues in Africa, I would guess a couple thousand people were there every night. As we presented our talks, we could look out all around the square and see people standing in their doorways, listening to everything that was said.

Here also, the children were waiting for us each afternoon when we arrived to set up our equipment. The pastors there had also made a large screen off to the right side of the platform onto which Bruce projected his pictures. We had a lovely movie on the life of Christ which we showed a ten-minute segment of each night. It was interesting to see the people cry and make sad sounds if something bad happened to Jesus, but when something good happened to Him they would laugh and clap. The last night we began early and showed the whole movie, and the people enjoyed it as much as the first time we had shown it to them.

Here the weather did not always cooperate with us. We had rain one night, the people just sat in the rain and listened anyway. Someone provided umbrellas for Bruce and me and for the projector. Another time the rain turned into a horrible storm. It blew down half of the screen on which the pictures were shown. It got so bad that someone invited Bruce and me to come and take shelter in one of closest small businesses by the platform. The storm soon passed and satan did not discourage us, so we went right back to finish our program. And those lovely people just patiently waited in the rain for it to pass and then enjoyed the rest of the presentation. The next afternoon someone came and fixed the screen, so everything was back to normal that night and no more rain. A bit of rain cannot dampen the desire of people to learn about the great love that Jesus has for us.

I had two different ladies who translated for me in Ghana. One of them asked us to please come to her home and pray for her husband. He was very sick and could no longer work to support his family. This family was having a rather hard time surviving. The people here were not wealthy. These people were not as poor as some other places we have been, but there were the poor and then a few very wealthy persons. There is usually no "middle class" in these countries.

We learned that there was a large gold mine right outside of the town we were in. Most of the men worked as miners in that mine. It was large and very productive, but mining for gold way underground in those conditions is hard work and very hard on the health of the miners. The husband whom we were invited to pray for had been a miner and because of the work had developed bad lung disease. We were told many people in town suffered the same thing. As often happens in third world countries, no provision had been made for those who became sick because of the work, and no provisions to provide help to their families when the men could no longer work to support their families.

One day we were invited to tour the gold mine. It was quite an interesting experience for us. We had to wear special boots the company gave us, we had to wear special hats with a light on each hat in case power was lost while we were down there, and most interesting to us was the fact that we each had to put on over our clothes, a white, cloth, full body coverall jump-suit type of garment. When the tour was over, we had to leave the shoes, hats, and coveralls there in a special room. Then each of us had to have an x-ray wand run all over our body to be sure that we had no gold or even gold dust on us. We asked if we could buy a small rock that might have a bit of gold in/on it just so we could have a souvenir to take home with us. We were told that was illegal, and if we did manage to buy it somewhere else it would be taken away from us at the airport before we left the country.

Ghana was another country which had a special name in their language for the Lord's Day, the seventh day of the week. The Ashanti people call the seventh day "memenda" which means "God's Day." God's name is "Onyame Kwame." His name means "He is God of the Sabbath" or "owner of the Sabbath Day."

In Ashanti "buroni" means "white." The first day of the week which we call Sunday is called "Kwasiada." The Ashanti people of Ghana call white people "Kwasi buroni" which means "white man who brought Sunday worship to Africa" because the priests from Spain who brought Sunday worship to them were white skinned compared to their black skins. This was very interesting to us.

We did enjoy the music in Africa. The people all love to sing. The people have their own tempo and method, but they really can sing, and we loved to hear them. There was usually no piano in the smaller churches but that is okay as the choir director (and all churches, no matter how small, have a choir) or the song leader sets the pitch, then he sings the first phrase or line of the song. He then stops and waits for the choir or the audience to sing that line. This is repeated for each phrase or line until the song is finished. Sometimes they also clap their hands and even move around a bit. It is just their way of praising God. However, when a person sings special music, the people do not think it is reverent to have any instrument accompany the singer.

One afternoon the pastor, his wife, and little girl about five years old came to visit us in our hotel room. As was my custom, I had made black puppets for the children in Ghana. I had these laying out on the bed as I was preparing for my puppet play that evening. The little girl was curious to see what our room looked like, I'm sure she had never been in a hotel room before and she just walked around exploring. When she came close to the bed, and she saw what looked to her, just like miniature, or shriveled up people she screamed and ran away from them. The puppets size was about fifteen inches from the tops of their heads to the bottom of their feet. I had made them to look like children who were the ages of the children for whom I was doing the program. The children really enjoyed the puppet plays, but having not seen a puppet before, much less four in a row, this little girl didn't know what those tiny people were for and what they were doing all lying in a row on the bed. It was obvious to her that those little people on the bed were not babies, they looked like young children and yet she had never seen such tiny, small children. They were so still, were they alive or not? She was frightened of them.

Nepal is a small country, sandwiched between India on the south, Tibet (which has been taken over by China) on the north, Bhutan is on its northeast corner, Pakistan on the west, and Myanmar (Burma) on the east. This country is very beautiful, the Himalayan mountains are all along its northern border. We were able to see Mt. Everest from our hotel room.

Our plane flew into the capital city of Kathmandu, and we were driven out to Bahnepa where our hotel was located and also the venue for our meetings. We were privileged to go to Nepal two different times, the first time in 2007 and the second in 2008. We learned to love the lovely people who lived there.

Nepal has been officially Hindu for many years, the Hindus have more gods than you can count, to foreigners, it is hard to recognize to which god the people should pray. Some of their gods are totally ugly, there is also a monkey god, an elephant god, a woman god with eight arms, some gods look like snakes, to our western eyes these gods just look ugly. Some of the people there have also begun to worship Buddha so in some of their worship places, there is a mixture of Hindu gods right alongside of Buddha. We saw some "gods" in little shrines along the road and even along the sidewalk in town which looked just like a piece of mal-formed cement. Yet, it was obvious this was a god because the people had left food, flowers, and red powder offerings beside it. There was also the necessary bell beside it.

The majority of the people live quite humbly and live very simply, but religion is a most important part of their everyday lives. I think what amazed us the most was that even though it is a very Hindu/Buddhist (pagan) country, they have some practices which come straight out of the Bible. How did this happen? We know that after Jesus arose from the dead and went back to heaven his disciples went to all corners of the then known world. Some of them went to India and parts of "Asia."

The Biblical teachings that the Nepalese follow had to have come from what the disciples taught them about Jesus and how He wants us to live. For example, our biggest surprise was that their work week, as well as their school week begins on the first day of the week, the day which the western world calls Sunday. The stores, schools, banks, and other businesses all close on the seventh-day Sabbath of the Bible. When you drive down the street on the seventh day you will see store after store shut up tightly and school children are everywhere, the banks are closed, and no one is around! On the first day of the week, Sunday, the banks are open, the children are in school, the shops are all open. Another interesting thing is that there are some extra-large goats running loose both in the country and in the cities. The people have herds of goats, but these are very different goats because they belong to no one. These goats do not hurt you, but they are not tame.

These goats are called "scape goats" that term comes straight from the Old Testament and was a part of the Jewish ceremonial law of forgiveness. How strange to hear the term, scapegoat, in a Hindu/Buddhist country. It seems that because the disciples went to Asia after Jesus went to heaven they would not have been teaching about the old Jewish system of sacrifice and forgiveness. Do you think maybe the wise men from the east who came to see baby Jesus took this teaching with them when they went back home? Or maybe some other dignitaries, just like the Ethiopian eunuch and the Queen of Sheba did when they went back to Africa. Maybe some other dignitaries from Asia went to Jerusalem and brought these beliefs to the people of Nepal. No one we asked seemed to know the origin of these goats, but everyone knew they were "scape goats" and no one touched them.

Another Biblical teaching is that the Nepali people will not eat pig because it is a filthy scavenger and is not safe for humans to eat. They do not even like to have anyone raise pigs around their homes because the pigs are so dirty and smelly, and the people do not want that smell close to them. As western ideas become more prevalent a very few people are beginning to raise pigs for some of the larger restaurants in large cities like Kathmandu, but the regular citizens do not appreciate having pigs anywhere around them or their land.

While I am talking about animals, I will mention that the Hindus do worship cows and think the cows are sacred (that is NOT Biblical!). The cows can wander anywhere all over the road in the country or in the city and if you are a driver of a vehicle, you dare not hit one of these cows for there would be a large penalty for doing so. The people do not even use cow's milk for things like yogurt, cheese, butter, etc. that we usually make from cow's milk. They use yak milk or buffalo milk for drinking, cooking, and making these other products. The people like ice cream and yogurt, but these are always made from yak or buffalo milk.

The Nepali people are very clean as a people. There is very little garbage or litter on their streets. Their houses are kept neat and clean. Their persons are also very clean. Many people do not have running water, especially out in the country, but the government has put pipes which contain running, clean water alongside of the road and you can see people taking this water home in large pots or even taking a bath under the pipe. They do this very modestly, their clothes are all left on their bodies, they just wash their bodies under their clothes, wash their hair at the same time, and then after their clothes are dry, they go on their way. They also wash their clothes in small basins in their homes and hang them outside to dry.

They always take their shoes off at the door when they come home, they do not want any street dirt coming into their homes. The people all take off their shoes at the front door of a church. When you visit a church, you just add your shoes to the pile that is already there. No one steals another person's shoes; each person just takes their own shoes when they go home. The people enter, and sit on a mat on the floor, but are very reverent and respectful towards God.

Their toilets are the typical Asian "squatty potties," just a hole in the floor, but these are kept quite clean also. There is usually a pair of flip-flops at the door to the bathroom so you can wear these when you go into the bathroom, and you don't have to get your feet "dirty" with anything that may have escaped when the person before you used the squatty potty.

Our meetings in Nepal were very well attended and the people loved to hear about the one all-powerful God and this God very kind and loving. The Hindu gods are vengeful, the real true God is loving and cares for His people. It used to be illegal to have public meetings in Nepal, but we were allowed to have public meetings, one time we used a large conference hall in the hotel where we were staying, the second time we even used the main hall in the public city hall. Even some of the city "big wigs" would stand at the door and listen. When we held meetings in the hotel the hotel workers would stand at the door or outside and listen as often as their work would allow. Including the two times we were in Nepal we actually held meetings at four different venues and always there was standing room only. It is such a blessing for the people to know that some god, out of who knows how many, is not vengefully waiting to punish you. There is just one God and He loves you and wants to take care of you. He only wants the best for you.

We were also blessed by being allowed to hold the very first ever public baptism. This we did in a river which ran along side of the main road outside of town goes up towards Tibet (China). While we were having the baptism two busloads of people stopped to watch, so it was certainly not a private thing. When a person finds out there is one, all-powerful God who loves and cares for His people, he or she has a very strong desire to return that love and this causes them to give their heart to Him. The water in this river came right out of the Himalayans and was very COLD.

Families would often have a business on the ground floor of a building and live upstairs. When a son got married, he would bring his wife to his home and after they had been married for a while and had their own family, his parents would add another floor above where the family lived, and the son and his wife would then live on that floor. The flat roof was used for drying crops like lentils, beans, rice, wheat, herbs, etc. The women also washed clothes on the roof and had clotheslines up there to dry the clothes. The man was definitely in charge of making the decisions for the family. The men would sit in a circle on the floor and the wife and daughters would serve the men first, when the men were satisfied, then the wife and daughters would sit on the floor, often in another room, and eat.

The wife could never be above her husband. While he sat on the floor to eat, she would have to stand in front of him, serve his food and pour his cup of drink. But she could not be "above" him. She could sit beside him if there was a sofa, or chairs but it was important that she not be higher than he was.

This fact was important in our meetings because we had people who wanted to tell where they were from and what their personal experience was. In our meetings everyone was treated alike and sat side by side, either on chairs or on the floor. One lady got up to tell how she came to the meetings.

She said she knew there were going to be meetings about Jesus, and she wanted to come very badly. Her husband said, "NO!" she could not go. His word was final. She kept asking and he totally denied her permission to come. Finally, as the day came nearer for the meetings to start, he took the dress she wore to go out in, and he hid it from her. She had nothing to wear, only had the rags which she wore to work around their home.

The day she should have left home, he lay down across the doorway, so she could not get out, and there he promptly fell asleep. The homes of the common people had only one or two rooms on the ground floor, some had a "loft" above. Sometimes the animals were kept inside on the ground floor and the people lived upstairs, over the animals. This home had only one level and one door. When the man was lying across the door sleeping, she could not get outside because she would have had to step over him and that would mean she was above him and higher than him.

She wanted to come and hear about this Jesus so badly that she finally just stepped over him and got outside. Once on her way, one of the other ladies at the meeting had loaned her a dress so that she could come to the meetings, but she was very frightened. She said please pray for me; my husband did not want me to come and because I had to step over him to get out of the house, he may kill me when I get home. I just had to hear about Jesus, but please pray for me when I must return home. When people have been worshipping gods who are vengeful, and then they learn about a loving, all-powerful God they will sacrifice all to learn as much as possible about Him and they want to follow Him completely.

We were taken to visit several of the Hindu temples in Nepal. We also visited some of the Buddhist temples there. The Buddhist temples had a very large Buddha's eye painted at the top, facing in each of the directions of the compass to remind people that Buddha sees everything in all directions. One of Buddhist the temples we visited was a very large one in the center of Kathmandu. The people were walking around the base of this temple, most people were walking fast. We were told this was because the more times that a person can go around the temple, the more blessing he or she will receive, so everyone walks fast so they can get around the temple as often as possible. We even saw some "priests" going around the temple on their stomachs. They would lie face down on the sidewalk, mark the spot where their head was, get up, put their feet where their head had been, and then lie face down again. This was their way of doing penance and earning extra favor with Buddha.

Prayer flags and prayer wheels are everywhere. These all come with prayers written on them. When the prayer flags flutter in the wind, the prayers supposedly ascend to the gods and are answered. Therefore, prayers can ascend all the time and you don't have to do anything more than hang the flags one time. The flags get very tattered because once up, it seems like they are left there until totally disintegrated. The "prayers" are written on the flags before you buy them.

Some prayer wheels are about three to four inches in diameter and the same in height. There is a cover on the little container which has a small weight attached to one spot. There is a little stick or post in the center at the bottom. As you walk along the street, you hold your prayer wheel in one hand by that little post and as you wave your hand in a circular motion, the little weight at one side of the cover causes the little container to spin around and around. Of course, the prayers are all written down on a long strip of paper which is placed inside of the container before you even buy the prayer wheel. The purchaser does not have to do anything. The prayers are all ready to go to the gods as you spin the wheel.

Always around temples and shrines, there are larger prayer wheels installed into niches built into the walls. As people walk past, they just reach out and flip their hand across the side of the prayer wheel which makes it spin around. There are several prayer wheels in a row (I did not stand and count them, but it looked like about ten of them), one in each niche, and all have the prayers already written in and on them. There is always some type of brass bell by the wheels and the person who wants their prayers heard always rings the bells to be sure his/her prayers are heard. I was reminded of the story in the Bible about Elijah on Mt. Carmel where he told the prophets of Baal to cry louder because maybe their gods were sleeping.

Some places had a whole room dedicated to a very large prayer wheel. This was quite a bit taller than a person and equally large in diameter. Here the person would have to walk around pulling on the prayer wheel to make it turn. This, too, had a large bell. All the shrines with idols, whether in a small, covered space at the side of the sidewalk, or whether in a large building dedicated just to the idol, had these bells. Larger idols had larger bells, smaller idols had smaller bells and sometimes there were several small bells. I always wondered if their gods were asleep and needed to be awakened. Since all the prayers are already printed on the flags or on paper inside of the prayer wheel before you buy it, I always wondered what if you want the gods to give you a certain thing and someone else wants the exact opposite for their request, and you are both spinning the same prayer wheel, how can the gods answer you both?

Another practice which was unique to us, was what happened when a person died, or was about to die. They practice cremation, and their belief is that the sooner you can get the ashes of your loved one into the Ganges River (which is holy to them), the sooner he/she will get his reward. Because of this belief they have what is called a burning ghat. This is a building with smaller rooms open to the river which are available for people to use If someone is sick and about to die the family brings their loved one to one of the ghats and puts them in a small room with their feet facing the river. Outside of this room is a cement platform, with wood and kindling already on it. We visited one such ghat in Kathmandu, and because it was a large city, they had several rooms. A priest (or priests) was standing around very close. As soon as the person dies the body is transferred to the cement platform.

The body is completely covered with a yellow cloth. The priest comes over and the family must pay him a fee to do the ceremony. While we were there, we saw a family place their loved one on the platform and cover the body, then the priest came over and wanted his fee. Evidently it was more than the family could pay or they knew the priest was asking too much money because it was obvious an argument ensued because by the waving of arms and the actions of both parties you could tell it was a very heated discussion. I felt so sorry for the family, to think their family member had just died and the spokesperson had to argue with the spiritual leader so that the ceremony could proceed.

The situation was finally settled, the priest sprinkled his yellow powder over the body, then he handed a torch to the oldest son of the family. The son had to walk around the cement platform three times, then he held the torch to the kindling until it caught fire, and the wood was burning well. The family stood around watching until the fire went out and only ashes were left. Then the priest took a large rake and scraped the ashes into the river which was right there. When the ashes were in the river, I noticed the priest reach up under his white garment and take off a pair of bright green underwear and toss it into the river! I don't know whether the last part was part of the ceremony or not.

The Ganges River is considered a holy river. It comes down from the Himalayan Mountains and flows into the sea. It was full of garbage. The people were standing at the edge bathing and washing their hair. The priests are considered "holy" men. Some of these priests just lived on the streets. They have no home or monastery, just the orange robe on their backs, their food was donated, their hair totally unkempt. These priests are called "street holy men." We saw one of the street "holy men" step into the river to clean himself, he scrubbed his bottom so hard you could tell it was caked with more than mud. Then the people take a drink of this water because it is supposed to bless them. It is a wonder anyone can survive after drinking the water from that river when you think of what all is in it. And this occurs not only in Kathmandu, but all along the length of the river. We were driven up to the border of China and saw ghats at several places along the river as it flowed down from higher up the mountain than Kathmandu. We also saw ghats south of Kathmandu as it flowed closer to India and the ocean.

It is good they use cremation as the country is small and mountainous and there would not be enough land to bury all the people. The complete burning is also much more sanitary than having diseased bodies all over the land. In times past there was a lot of leprosy in Nepal. There is still some, but now there is a cure for that terrible disease and there are sanitariums where the lepers can go to be cured.

We had ex-lepers at our meetings, since the people all take their shoes off at the door it was easy to see the crippled feet, with no toes, and see the hands with no fingers. But now the people were cured and could safely live in society.

There was a young lady (late teens or early twenties) at our meetings. She was a very kind girl and offered to help me translate for the children. She was such a kind person and had such a talent for dealing with the children. We discovered that she had had to leave school to care for her father who was a leper. He must have died before we got to know her because we never saw him, and she was no longer taking care of him. She wanted to go back to school but had no money for the tuition. We offered to help pay for her schooling at a Christian boarding school in India as there was no Christian school in Nepal. She gratefully accepted our offer and today she is a teacher at that college. She is also married and a mother.

No, we are/were not wealthy to be able travel all over the world on mission trips or to pay for people's college education. Tuition is much cheaper there than it is here. Also, it took quite a bit of sacrifice on our part, but we enjoyed helping others. No matter how little we have, it is still much more than most people in the world have. For over fifty years Bruce and I cut each other's hair, not a huge sum, but it adds up over time. And after some early mistakes, we learned how to do it.

We could have a lot more money to share and to use helping others if we washed our own hair, rather than going to the beauty parlor and having it washed and styled for us every week. What if we saved the money spent on fancy to-go coffees? What if we just got the extra special things once a week? What if we skipped the sodas, or drinks while eating out and just drank water. What if we didn't eat out so often? How much could we give if we did not buy that new pair of shoes another knick-knack for the house? It would be easy to list many more things, but each of us has to make our own decisions as to how we use our resources. Those decisions should be made knowing that God is keeping track of all our thoughts and actions.

As Bruce and I went on these trips to different countries around the world, we never went as "tourists," but as missionaries. We certainly enjoyed it and had a lot of interesting experiences but that was never our first goal. We were just trying to do our little bit to fulfil what Jesus told those who love Him to do. Matt.28:19,20.

I just stop to think of what Jesus sacrificed for us and the humble way He lived while on earth and it makes me want to do all I can to bring more people to love and serve Him. I also think of the illustration in the Bible which Jesus gave about the woman who cast her two mites into the offering container. I remember the extremely poor widow in my time who gave her food for one day so that she could bring an offering to church with her. Then there is the man, also in my day, who cut trees in the forest to support his family. He would then chop the trees up and sell the firewood. His offering for God each week was the profits of the firewood which he sold on one day of the week.

It is not whether we can "afford" it or not, it is how much we could do for others, the amount we choose to keep for our own use and pleasure.

When we checked into our hotel in Bahnepa there were several candles on the desk. It looked odd, but we soon found out that there were regular power outages. The power outages were never predictable and could last up to two hours, so the hotel provided candles, so we did not have to sit in the dark. During wintertime they would come around in the evening and lend us a kerosene heater so we could have warmth. We tried not to use this kerosene heater any more than necessary as it did not smell very good in a small, closed room.

Early during our meetings in Nepal, we had some interesting guests. One day two Tibetan priest/teachers came walking into the meeting. These Tibetan priest/teachers are called lamas. They were dressed in their full Tibetan lama garb of maroon robes, trimmed in gold and blue, so it was easy to tell who they were. We never found out how they heard about our meetings in Bahnepa, the city where we were in, which was east of Kathmandu. These lamas told us they had come from a mountain high up in Tibet (China). They had walked as fast as they could for a whole day to get down to the road where the "bus" passed. Someone told us that a good American hiker would have had to hike at a good clip for three days to cover the amount of ground that these two men covered in one full day!

When the bus came, they got on it and rode another full day to arrive in Kathmandu. There the lamas planned to catch a bus and ride out to Bahnepa. But to their consternation they discovered that Kathmandu was in the middle of a bus strike. The two of them decided that since they had already walked so far and made such an effort to get to the meetings, they would not give up now but would walk the forty or so miles out to Bahnepa. As they were walking along, a man in a car drove past and recognized that they were lamas by their clothes, so he stopped and offered to give them a ride out to Bahnepa. That is how two lamas came to our meetings. Several years later we heard that there was a small group of people worshiping Jesus high back up in the mountains of Tibet (China).

While we were in Nepal on our second trip to that lovely country, there was an upheaval in the government. The communists came in and overthrew the Hindu King and put a communist president in charge of the country. This was not a good thing for the Nepalese people. The road which went close to our hotel and was the main road between Nepal and China (ex-Tibet), was a good place for the communists to demonstrate their powers. This was part of what had been called the old Silk Road. One day the communists put on a demonstration and the road was covered with people walking and demonstrating, from one side of the road to the other side as far as we could see, this blocked all cars, buses, trucks, and other people who walked along there to do their daily business. When these types of things happen, it is best for you to stay away and in your house, in our case, the hotel where we were staying, until they are done with their demonstration.

The pastor who was the leader of the group of believers where we were meeting took us up into the mountains, very close to the border of China. There was a small church there which he wanted us to visit. It was quite primitive, but the people loved Jesus and it was a real privilege to meet with them. The communists had not been happy to see a church there, because when there is a church teaching about Jesus, the communists cannot control the people as well as when there is no religion. Because the communists did not want religion and churches in that area, they bombed the church, half of it was totally destroyed, but the people had patched up the remaining part as best they could and were still meeting in the part which was left standing. We had a lovely meeting with them that day and they were so greatly encouraged to know that "outsiders" really cared for them.

We were always happy when we got to have meetings in Spanish-speaking countries because then we did not need a translator and we felt more comfortable and at home. This was true everywhere except Venezuela, I won't say much about our time there except that we were made sad by what we observed. The communists were trying hard to take over that country and it had become control by anarchy. There was quite a bit of anti-American sentiment at that time. There also we had about an hour's drive to our venue, not because of distance but because it was mostly through the city, heavy with traffic.

Our driver knew we were both fluent in Spanish; however, he chose to keep his radio tuned to a Spanish station which broadcast communist ideals and anti-Americanism the whole time. That was a different experience for us. The road was three lanes wide in each direction, but there were four lanes of traffic because the people drove wherever they wanted, one shoulder of the road to the other shoulder of the road, and the motorcycles would squeeze between the vehicles by putting one hand on the vehicle at whichever side was closest and push themselves along.

We did have a very happy encounter while there. When Bruce's and my parents worked in Colombia in the 1940's there was a Venezuelan family there who had three children, two girls and a boy. The girls were my playmates even though they were both a little older than I was. By the time Bruce and I went to Venezuela, their father had retired and died, but the mother and her three children had returned to Venezuela and were living in Caracas which was the city we were in.

The oldest daughter had become an obstetrician and was in charge of the largest maternity hospital in the city of Caracas. She owned a nice home on the outskirts of the city. The youngest daughter was a dentist with a good practice in town and she lived in a lovely high-rise apartment in the city. Both girls (now women) were very frightened at what was happening in their country because of communism coming in. The doctor being a bit farther out of the city felt a bit safer, but the dentist was not safe. Her office had two outside doors. The outer one opened onto the street but was locked 100% of the time. A patient had to ring a bell and identify themselves. Someone inside would push a button and the door would click open. The patient could then walk "inside" and was "trapped" in a small narrow hallway. Someone who worked inside would peek out a small window and identify that it really was the patient, and that he or she was alone and then the worker would push a button that unlocked the inner door. A very insecure and frightening way to work.

The dentist invited us to her home for a meal. She came and picked us up and drove us to her building. The parking garage was under the high-rise apartment building, and she had to use a security code to open the metal door to the garage. She then parked in her spot, and we walked to the elevator. She had to use another security code to open the elevator door. Once we reached her floor, we walked down the hallway and came to another security door where she had to use another code. When that opened, we stepped inside and there was one door to the right, her neighbors, and one door to the left, her door. She had to then use her own key to open the door to her apartment.

Both of these women were afraid they were going to lose their homes. When you live under anarchy, and have something, whoever wants to take what you have can do it if they are stronger than you are. Each person is their own personal law and follows their personal desires. That is an immensely unsecure, frightening way to live.

When I was a young child (so young I can't remember when) I memorized Psalms 34:7, the angel of the Lord encamps all around those who love Him and delivers them, what a blessing! Jesus has intervened and or protected me during my lifetime more times than I can count. I can never thank Him enough.

Elsie, my mother, who was told as a child that she was ugly and stupid and would never amount to anything, honored God all during her entire adult life. Not only that, but she also had a very strong influence on my life as she taught me to love and serve Jesus. Her example inspired me to do so much for the children everywhere we went. Children are so impressionable; their little minds absorb much more than most adults think they do. When a child gives his or her heart to God there is a whole lifetime ahead of them to honor God. An adult's mind is often made up already and if a positive change is made, their life is at least half used up. But it is always better to give God half of your life, than none of it!

This was strongly brought home to me as Bruce, and I were driving home from church with our young children one week. The sermon that week had been something about the sacrificial ceremonies of the children of Israel. I remember thinking to myself how are the children going to be helped by this sermon, what can they understand about it? Our oldest son was four years old at the time and he was standing behind Bruce as we drove home (we did not have seat belts or safety car seats at that time and children could move around as they desired). Suddenly, out of the blue he asked, "Daddy, if the Jews do not believe in Jesus now, why don't they still offer lamb sacrifices for their sins?" Wow! Never underestimate the understanding of what a child sees and hears.

One of Bruce's and my favorite Bible texts is Isaiah 49:25 where God says He will fight against the one who fights against us (the evil one) and He will save our children.

Many years ago, I found a short poem, written by a lady who had been a missionary in Nepal many years before Bruce and I visited there.

Exquisite Moment

To be able to stand,
Hand in hand with your mate,
Side by side with your children,
Before Him, and say,
"Here am I and the children.
You have given me!"
O, moment, most exquisite
In all eternity.

- Barbara Sturgess

One of the ways that Elsie, my mother, honored God in her life was the work she did for children. That work and the influence of her life continues to honor Him today.

Chris is the little boy sitting on his daddy's lap.

Chris and Lydia's wedding picture, 1915. Many years after Elsie was married and after the death of Grandpa Daniel and Grandma Carolina, someone from their family gave this picture to Elsie.

The house which Chris built for his bride. The outhouse is the small building at the back.

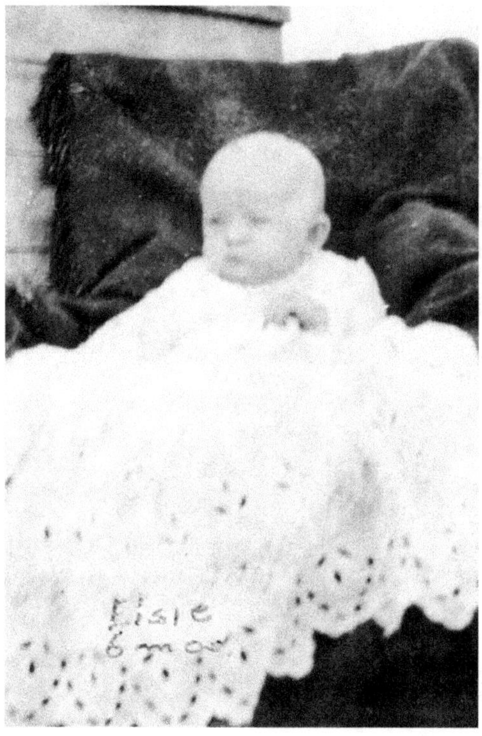

Elsie at six months of age.

Irene, on the left, and Elsie.
This is the only known picture of Irene.

Elsie, four years old in the front yard.
The schoolhouse would later be built on the other
side of the shrubbery behind her.

Posing for a formal portrait, Elsie at five years of age.

Melvina enjoying her bath in the kitchen wash-up sink beside the back door.

Three little "orphans" about the time Papa went on his trip.

Andrew Riley, the man who wrote the letter requesting that someone be sent to help his family understand the Bible.

Grandpa Daniel and Grandma Carolina

Sam and Lydia's wedding picture, 1914.
She was just 17 years old. He was 22 years old.

Sam and Lydia with Lloyd as a baby (1915). Sam was trying to be a farmer as his father Andrew told him he must be.

Sam as a young minister and Lydia (1915).
Lloyd was 4 ½ years old.

Elsie and Lloyd's wedding, June 6, 1937.

Elsie with her two daughters beside the car that took their family up and over the Andes Mountains and then back home again.

About the Author

Carol is Elsie's oldest daughter. She has a deep love for reading and collecting true stories, and she enjoys sharing these stories with others. Carol graduated from Michigan State University in Lansing, Michigan. While there, she gratefully accepted the invitation to join Phi Kappa Phi and Omicron Nu, two honors societies. Over the years, Carol has published two short stories and has written numerous skits for the puppets she created. She was married to the love of her life for 65 years, and they were blessed with two daughters and two sons. She is a Christian who loves God with her whole heart and enjoys sharing His love with others. *The Lady Who Chose Joy* is her first book.

www.ingramcontent.com/pod-product-compliance
Lightning Source LLC
LaVergne TN
LVHW050628100826
845148LV00011B/1773

* 9 7 8 0 9 6 6 8 6 2 2 4 9 *